globaliz...

on trial

The world was once thought to be flat, then proved
to be round. Now it is quite definitely web shaped!

— Anonymous

A world civilization could, in fact, represent
more than a worldwide coalition of cultures,
each of which would preserve its own originality.

— Claude Levi-Strauss

All Adam's children are members of the same frame:
Since all, at first from the same essence came.
When by hard fortune one limb is oppressed:
The other members lose their wonted rest.
If thou feel'st not for others' misery:
A child of Adam is no name for thee.

— Sheikh Moslehadin Sa'di

globalization
on trial

The Human
Condition and
the Information
Civilization

Farhang Rajaee

© International Development Research Centre 2000

Published in Canada by the International Development Research Centre
PO Box 8500, Ottawa, ON, Canada K1G 3H9
http://www.idrc.ca/books/

Published in Europe and the United States of America by Kumarian Press Inc.
14 Oakwood Avenue, West Hartford, Connecticut 06119-2127, USA
http://www.kpbooks.com/

Canadian Cataloging in Publication Data

Rajaee, Farhang, 1952–
Globalization on trial : the human condition and the information civilization

Includes bibliographical references and index.
ISBN 0-88936-909-7

1. Information society. 2. International economic relations. 3. Democracy. 4. Nationalism. 5. Education, Higher. I. International Development Research Centre (Canada) II. Title.

HD221.F37 2000   301   C00-980008-5

Library of Congress Cataloging-in-Publication Data

Rajaee, Farhang, 1952–
    Globalization on trial : the human condition and the information
        civilization / Farhang Rajaee.
            p. cm.
    Includes bibliographical references and index.
    ISBN 1-56549-111-4 (pbk.)
    1. International relations. 2. International cooperation. 3. Information technology. I. Title.

JZ1318.R35 2000
303.48'33—dc21   99-089900

09 08 07 06 05 04 03 02 01 00   10 9 8 7 6 5 4 3 2 1   1st printing 2000

Contents

Foreword

In the new information age, we are faced with a daily deluge of new facts from an ever-widening set of sources on an ever-widening set of subjects. At a premium are those few sources that attempt to make sense of this great transition, not only in providing an interpretation of what has happened and why but also in offering a vision of what might be done to develop a more humane future. This all-too-brief monograph by Dr Farhang Rajaee provides us with a critical overview of the principal (and often competing) interpretations of the complex phenomena labeled globalization, as well as a vision of the future. He has drawn on a broad range of sources — Western and non-Western, optimistic and pessimistic — in grappling with the many economic, political, and cultural dimensions of the growing global interdependence. Most of all, he is concerned with what kind of education will be needed to cope with the increasingly complex challenges of the information age.

We have already witnessed a dramatic increase in both the numbers of courses and the types of education for essentially technological careers in the information age — in engineering and computer science and in business management. Technological innovation has, after all, been the hallmark of Western civilization, and those who can cope most effectively with technology have played key roles in both creating and managing change. Dr Rajaee reminds us, however, that severe crises in social organization and values have accompanied previous periods of such intensive technological change, and he reminds us of the twin dangers of excessive resistance to change and excessive celebration of the new. On the basis of ancient Greek philosophy, as well as his own research on ancient Eastern philosophy, he reminds us of the importance of balance and of seeing that the opposites — "us and them," unity and diversity, technology and the humanities — are often complementary and not contradictory. To provide just such a sense of balance was, historically, the role of the university, but in an age of increasing complexity and division of labour, the university itself has been deeply marked by fragmentation, almost to the point at which its enormous success in generating technological and scientific innovation has undermined its contribution to philosophy, the humanities, and the social sciences. All too often, it is in the most advanced technological sectors where fundamentalist political and religious movements find their most devoted followers, which is one of the least understood ironies of these twin processes of technological innovation and social fragmentation.

Dr Rajaee envisions a restoration of dialogue and the emancipation of humanity through communication across and within the major world civilizations. Dr Rajaee's vision contains a deep moral commitment to human worth and dignity, as shared by the major world religious faiths, as well as by secular humanists. In this vision, we need to go beyond the "either—or" system of categories for judging others and understand "both—and" if we are to learn from each other at a time when highly innovative societies are undergoing deep social fragmentation and excessively traditional societies are suffering in poverty and decay. In Dr Rajaee's view, we are engaged, perhaps for the first time, in simultaneous processes of deep change in which shared information and communication, on a truly global scale, offer enormous potential for human emancipation, provided we understand both the opportunities and the dangers.

John Sigler
Carleton University
January 2000

Preface

Some years ago, the political scientist and philosopher Hannah Arendt (1906–75) thought that an event in 1957 had changed the human condition forever: a Soviet Earth-orbiting satellite communicated pictures of the Earth never seen before. The Canadian thinker Marshall Herbert McLuhan (1911–80) predicted that the advancement of communication would make a global village of humanity scattered across the five continents. This has become a reality as the World Wide Web has connected the four corners of the world. This process has been termed globalization. But has globalization truly increased understanding among peoples and led to mutual appreciation and respect? The question at the heart of this book is this: What is the human condition in the global age? Implicit in McLuhan's prediction is an optimism about humanity's potential for living together in harmony, and I share most of this optimism. Indeed, four decades ago, when I left my village in Iran in search of education, knowledge, and self-fulfillment, my most important asset was my faith in human goodness.

My journey has taken me to many places and provided me with opportunities to meet people of various cultures. I have run across many whose hearts warm when they truly communicate with another human being. Time and again, I have witnessed how barriers of ethnicity, nationality, race, religion, and culture crumble in the face of such encounters. Dialogue and understanding are building blocks for the betterment of humanity. The very existence of such people bears out my optimism and serves as a signpost for others to follow a similar path.

It has been my good fortune to have my professional and personal ideals follow the same trajectory. As a political scientist and, more specifically, a theoretician of international relations, I ponder over the perennial question of how one can reconcile the infinite desires and ambitions of humanity with the finitude of available material resources. Great masters, such as Aristotle, have taught us that the solution depends on how we collectively order our lives. Hannah Arendt reminded us that this, in turn, depends on how successfully we interact and communicate with one another. As a member of the species *Homo sapiens*, I desire to communicate with others, despite cultural, religious, and political differences and prejudices. The information and communication age has provided the means to achieve this communication and, more importantly, reduced the significance of boundaries.

An invitation I recently received to participate in the globalization project of the Zentrum Moderner Orient, in Berlin, was fortuitously timely for me. While in Germany I found the academic debate at the institute sharpened my perception of the issues and consequences of globalization. But more interesting was the experience of living in a post-Cold War Western metropolis, a united Berlin. The enormous inflow of people, particularly from Eastern Europe, and the reconstruction of Berlin — not by the German federal government, but mainly by a host of multinational corporations, such as Sony and others — made me realize that a major revolution was taking place. The world is truly becoming one globe. Even the Islamic movements, the subject of my ongoing research, which I had originally thought had risen out of the internal logic of Islamic civilization, are, as I discovered, related to the globalization process.

The post-Cold War transformation of world politics has generated the paradox of the global–local interface. At one level, this transformation as it occurs in Berlin is a very local German phenomenon, but at another it is a very global one. This paradox seems to be the most intriguing feature of globalization. It is fascinating, therefore, to examine the ways in which globalism and nativism feed on each other, modify one another, and strike a balance. I feel that the survival of the one depends on the other. In this essay, I examine the human condition from the angle of globalization but consider localization insofar as it helps to explain globalization.

The need for further research on the topic took me from Berlin to Ottawa, Canada, where I had an opportunity to teach at Carleton University. This provided me with further opportunities to discuss some of my hypotheses with peers and critics. Although the Chinese proverb "teaching is the best device of learning" is correct, teaching alone, without research, has its limitations. The opportunity to debate with peers and critics and to have a base and support for research — to decipher and digest the arguments — should complement the process of teaching and learning. I have been fortunate to have also enjoyed such opportunities at other academic institutions, such as the Miller Center of Public Affairs of the University of Virginia, Paul H. Nitze School of Advanced International Studies of Johns Hopkins University, the Royal Military College of Canada, Shawnee State University, and Youngstown State University, which each provided me with a forum for presentation and exchange of ideas.

The International Development Research Centre (IDRC), in Ottawa, provided the financial support for the research presented in this book, and the College of the Humanities at Carleton University provided the research base. I am deeply indebted to Kenneth W. Thompson, Fouad Ajami, Houchang Hassan-Yari, John Lorentz, Keith John Lepak, Pierre Beemans, and Peter C. Emberely for their invaluable assistance. I wish also to further acknowledge the support of IDRC, which not only funded the original research in the 1998/99 academic year but also extended its support for the summer of 1999 to enable me to revise the text. I would like to thank some other individuals, whose unfailing encouragement influenced the work and helped me finish it. John Sigler has been a good friend, a counselor, and an insightful critic. Christopher C. Smart showed how truly he is a friend, insightful observer, and lover of truth. My dialogue with Tom Darby on the nature of the globalization process never stopped and always helped me to clarify my thought. Father William F. Ryan was kind enough to discuss many of the issues with me and raise important questions. Kazem Sajjadpour, together with another friend, who wishes to remain anonymous, suggested that I should delve into the nature of globalization as a phenomenon.

I also wish to acknowledge the encouragement, help, and criticism of the following individuals: David Brooks, Inis Claude, Jr, Jan-Georg Deutsch, Henner Furtig, M.R. Ghanoonparvar, Fatemeh Givechian, Jabbar Khan, Gregory MacIsaac, Ken McGillivray, Vincent Mosco, Mehdi Mozaffari, Walter Randy Newell, David Symons, Warren Thorngate, Achim Von Oppen, Harold Von Riekhoff, Craig Waggaman, and Tom Wilkinson.

During my research trip to Iran in the summer of 1998, I enjoyed discussing the topic with many people, to all of whom I am grateful. I would especially like to thank the philosopher Gholamhossein Ibrahimi Dinani and the theologian and Islamic reformer Mohammad Mojtahid Shabestari for sharing their views with me. Ali Mojtahid was kind enough to arrange for me to give a lecture for his colleagues at the Ministry of Foreign Affairs.

Five anonymous readers examined the text before its final revision, and I am grateful to each of them. Their words of encouragement were the best reward, and their sharp and insightful questions provided me with new ways to rework, reconstruct, and elaborate on some parts of the text. I am indebted to each one and have incorporated most of their suggestions. I would also like to thank IDRC Books, and particularly Bill Carman, and Kumarian Press, and particularly Linda Beyus, for showing encouragement and enthusiasm for my work.

A few words about the title are in order. I began with *One Civilization — Many Civilizations,* which was very revealing of the main feature of the new human civilizational phase: it reveals how globalization contains many civilizations, each of which may define the new mode of production in its own terms. However, this title fails to capture the consequences and the implications of the globalization process, as presented in this work. The new title, *Globalization on Trial,* allows some degree of flexibility, and it opens the debate on many aspects of the process. On reading the earlier manuscript, Tom Darby directed my attention to the relevance of Jean Bethke Elshtain's *Democracy on Trial* (1995) to my work. I had seen the book before, but on revisiting it, I agreed with Darby's insight. Elshtain's work, which she originally delivered as the 1993 Massey Lectures, examines the nature and limitations of democracy in America. Similarly, in this work I examine the nature and consequences of globalization for the human community. Many of Elshtain's comments on the responsibilities of a citizen in a democratic society have direct bearing on the responsibilities of a global citizen in the new information society. I discuss some of her insights in Chapters 3 and 5.

The central thesis of this book is that the combination of the fall of the bipolar world system, the coming of the information revolution, and the emergence of postmodernist thinking has ushered in a new epoch. Its new mode of production challenges existing views and requires an imaginative mode of thinking. The existing paradigms do not completely grasp the nature, the consequence, and the implication of the present transformation. Yet, because the other important variable of the equation — namely, humanity — has remained relatively unchanged and still requires a life of security, welfare, and dignity, this imaginative thinking requires a holistic view that accounts for both change and continuity. The transformation of the material-life world has presented both challenges and opportunities. It is incumbent on humanity to exercise ingenuity and devise a new mechanism for global governance, one that responds to these challenges and takes advantage of the opportunities. This book presents my understanding of these challenges and suggests some responses to them.

I have presented my argument in four chapters. The first sets the stage for the presentation and explains the work's theoretical approach and methodology. Chapter 2 contextualizes the position I have taken on the nature of globalization, comparing this with other paradigms prevalent among scholars and practitioners. It puts forward a complex theory of human nature and its relation to civilizational contexts in general and to the information civilizational context inaugurated by globalization. Chapter 3 presents my understanding of the nature of the emerging information civilization. It argues that this new phase in human history involves the paradox of "one civilization — many civilizations," with technology as its theoretical base; information, its mode of production; and pluralism, its operational feature. This chapter further evaluates the possibility of dialogue or clash among the various components of this new civilization. It suggests that humanity can either encourage conflict or foster dialogue, depending on its political will, wisdom, and foresight. Chapter 4 outlines the challenges the new civilization presents and suggests possible responses or areas for further research. Like all civilizational epochs, this one has the potential for both positive and negative consequences. Finally, in Chapter 5, given as a short conclusion, I draw some general lessons for the future.

All dates in this essay are given according to the Christian calendar, even those of non-Western thinkers.

Farhang Rajaee
Carleton University
January 2000

CHAPTER 1

The New Creation

The Earth is the very quintessence of the human condition.
— Arendt (1958, p. 2)

A NEW WORLD IN THE MAKING

"When there is a general change of conditions, it is as if the entire creation had changed and the whole world had been altered, as if it were a new and repeated creation, a world brought into existence anew" (Ibn Khaldun 1958, vol. I, p. 65). This is how, in 1377, the perceptive philosopher of history, Ibn Khaldun (1332–1406), began his magnum opus on the rise and fall of civilization.[1] He made this observation based, first, on the general turbulence of this era in the history of North Africa and Andalusia and then, and more importantly, on the Mongol invasion of his Islamic civilizational milieu, which had

---

[1] Abd al-Rahman Ibn Mohammad, generally known as Ibn Khaldun, was born in Tunis in 1332. His was a distinguished family of originally Yemenite Arabs who had settled in Spain, but who, after the fall of Seville, had migrated to Tunisia. At an early age, he entered public life at the service of the Egyptian ruler, Sultan Barquq. But his political career was not very successful, and a long period of unrest, marked by political rivalries, made him take refuge in the small village Qalat Ibn Salama in Algeria, where he wrote *The Muqaddimah*, the first volume of his world history. He spent the last 24 years of his life in Egypt, a life of fame and respect, as the Chief Malakite Judge and as a lecturer at Al-Azhar University.

disrupted the existing order. Apparently, Ibn Khaldun had a personal encounter with the Mongol conqueror, Tamerlane (*Timur Lang*, 1336–1405), outside of Damascus. The conqueror even sought Ibn Khaldun's advice and collaboration.

However, Ibn Khaldun was more interested in understanding this "new creation" and the cause of the decline of the former civilization (Mahdi 1957). His civilizational milieu's inability to respond to the challenges of the day indicated the coming of a new era. As a keen observer of events, Ibn Khaldun wanted to understand and explain the reasons for this historical change, as he thought the existing paradigms could not explain the event. His was an exercise with the dual aim of understanding the conditions in the past leading up to the contemporary situation and of formulating guidelines for future action. "Therefore, there is a need at this time," he wrote, "that someone should systematically set down the situation of the world among all regions and races" (Ibn Khaldun 1958, vol. 1, p. 65). He was aware that this was a recurring process. As the Greek philosopher Heraclitus (535–475 BCE) had suggested in his famous phrase "you cannot step twice into the same river," change is an integral part of life, and one's response to change should be to formulate a new paradigm to make sense of it. Ibn Khaldun did just that. In his own words, he was "doing for his age what al-Mus'udi [a previous historian had done] for his. This should be a model for future historians to follow" (Ibn Khaldun 1958, vol. 1, p. 65).

Ibn Khaldun attempted to answer what Aristotle had identified as the core question of public life, "How do we order our life together" so as to guarantee the good life, which is the "the chief end, both for the community as a whole and for each of us individually?" (Aristotle 1958, 1278b). Ibn Khaldun called his paradigm *al-'Emran*, the "science of civilization" (Ibn Khaldun 1958, vol. 1, pp. 83–84). *Al-'Emran* not only explained the contemporary situation but also suggested a broad pattern for any future order. The destruction of the Islamic empire suggested to Ibn Khaldun that the centuries-old caliphate system had lost its relevance. Instead, broader intellectual paradigms were needed to ensure any future order. Coincidentally, internal and external challenges, such as the Crusades and the rise of the Shi'i Isma'ilis, had led Muslims such as Imam Muhammad Ghazali (*d.* IIII) (Ghazali 1978) and, later, Ibn Taymiyyah (1263–1328) (Ibn Taymiyyah 1966) to work out theories for what Iqbal later called the "reconstruction of religious science" (Iqbal 1951, chapter I). Ibn Taymiyyah suggested that a revised theory of politics should henceforth restore the Islamic message as formulated in the Islamic law, the *Shari'a*, rather than relying on the authority of the person in charge of Islamic polity, which was the main point of Ibn Taymiyyah's theory of *al-Siyasa al-Share'ya* (the *Shari'a*-based politics) (Bannan 1988).

3

The life experiences of many great thinkers have indicated this recurring theme — the formulation of a paradigm in response to an all-out crisis.[2] The Athenian Plato (427?–347 BCE), the Chinese Confucius (551–479 BCE), the Indian Kautilya (in the 4th century BCE), the Iranian Mazdak (in the 5th century), and the Bishop of Hippo, St Augustine (354–430), did for their respective civilizations what Ibn Khaldun was to do centuries later for his own. In modern times, the Italian statesman and thinker Niccolo Machiavelli (1469–1527), the English philosophers Thomas Hobbes (1588–1679) and John Locke (1632–1704), the French philosopher Jean-Jacques Rousseau (1712–78), the German philosophers Georg Wilhelm Friedrich Hegel (1770–1831) and Karl Marx (1818–83), and others were to do the same. "The owl of Minerva spreads its wings only with the falling of the dusk," wrote Hegel (1942, p. 13), in his work *The Philosophy of Right*. More importantly, in the preface to his *Phenomenology of Mind*, in 1806, Hegel talked about the coming of a new world: "it is not difficult to see that our epoch is a birth-time, and a period of transition ... in a flash and at a single stroke, [it] brings to view the form and structure of the new

---

[2] In a thoughtful and thought-provoking book, *Understanding Political Theories* (Spragens 1976), Thomas Spragens, Jr showed how great theories have been formulated in response to all-out crises and disorder.

world" (Hegel 1967, p. 75). The American thinker, Walter Lippmann, expressed the same idea in the early 20th century, when he wrote, "I began writing a book in an effort to come to terms in my own mind and heart with the mounting disorder in our Western society" (Lippmann 1956, p. 11). Lippmann and other thinkers have all attempted to come to terms with the mounting disorder of their respective societies and to suggest ways to bring order back to human life.

Why introduce an inquiry into the human condition in the information age with the thought of a 14th-century Muslim scholar? The first reason is that Ibn Khaldun's time and world greatly resembled our own. The Mongol invasion destroyed his political context. The hegemonic authority of the caliph, which was universally recognized, had ordered the world of Ibn Khaldun: even the minority Shi'is, for whom the ideal authority was the rule of an infallible and divinely ordained leader (*imam*), and not the caliph, acknowledged the latter as sovereign.[3] Similarly, our Westphalian state system has lost much of its legitimacy and efficiency today. The hegemonic structure that kept the balance of powers and the world order has been shaken. I am using *hegemony* as defined by Robert Cox: "a structure of values and understanding about the nature of order that permeates a whole system of states and non-state entities" (Cox 1992, p. 140). Globalization has undermined the hegemonic order of the Westphalian state system, and here lies the second reason to consider Ibn Khaldun's ideas. His treatment of the changed situation as a "new creation" provides us with a model to use in examining our posthegemonic world. He also invented a new science, the science of civilization (*al-'Emran*), to make sense of the emerging world order of his time.

The information revolution heralds a new epoch. The series of events marking the last decades of the millennium have indicated that we may also be confronting a new creation. These events all happened in the year 1989, which in hindsight,

---

[3] There is an important distinction between "power" and "authority." Although the actual power of the caliph fluctuated, depending on the period in Islamic history, his authority was at all times recognized and accepted.

proved to be a watershed. What were they? (1) The Berlin Wall fell; (2) Ayatollah Ruhoullah Imam Khomeini (1902–89) died; (3) the Soviet Union's aid to Cuba ceased; (4) Violeta Barrios de Chamorro defeated the Sandanista revolutionary Daniel Ortega Saavedra; (5) female students in France challenged the secular educational system by wearing the traditional Muslim headscarf in public schools (the country's highest administrative body, the Conseil d'État [council of state] defended the students' right to practice their religion); and (6) the most important of all, Tim Berners-Lee invented the World Wide Web, the Internet-based hypermedia initiative for global information sharing. The first event marked the end of the bipolar world.[4]

5

No longer has humanity only two "systems" to choose from, socialism and capitalism — the arena is now open to a greater variety of ways for people to enhance their opportunities. The second event eroded the transnationalist aspects of the Islamic movements: in less than a decade after the death of the leader of the revolution, in the fall of 1998, the Iranian government disassociated itself from the *fatwa* on the life of the British writer Salman Rushdie, who had been found guilty of insulting Muslims and their religion (Mozaffari 1998b). The third development signified the end of support for the liberation movements and revolutions in Latin America — the Soviet Union started to behave as a nation-state, rather than an empire. The fourth event marked the emergence of the power of civil society in a region hitherto cursed with "junta politics" of one form or another. The fifth incident clearly showed that the metanarrative of modernity and the Enlightenment project has lost its monopoly as a paradigm. The sixth event formed the most potent framework for the emergence of the information revolution: the World Wide Web opened a new arena hitherto unknown to humanity. What linked these apparently unrelated

---

[4] "Bipolar world" refers to the organization of the world from the end of World War II (1939–45) until the fall of the Soviet empire in 1989. The world was divided between the allied forces of noncommunist countries under the leadership of the United States of America, symbolized by the North Atlantic Treaty Organization (NATO), and the communist countries under the leadership of the Soviet Union, symbolized by the Warsaw Pact.

events was a result of the Pentagon's decision in 1990 to decommission the Advanced Research Projects Agency network (ARPANET), thereby opening hyperspace to the entire world. This gave rise to a new phase in human history.

Symbolically, three events should be singled out as main indicators of the new creation: the fall of the Soviet Union, the death of Khomeini, and the emergence of the Internet. The first two have an important common feature. Both mark the end of apparently opposite and, in any case, extreme ways of thinking. The fall of the Soviet Union marks the failure and rejection of extreme secularism and a materialist worldview, whereas the death of Khomeini ended exclusive religiosity and theocracy. Both the secular and the religious one-dimensional views of humanity, nature, and the world proved inadequate for the challenges humanity faces today. The third event, the birth of the Internet, brought the promise of a new way of thinking and a new sphere for both the *vita activa* and the *vita contemplativa* (the active life and the contemplative one), to recall the concepts used by Hannah Arendt (1957).[5] The birth of the Internet could not have come about without the melding of communications hardware and the software of computer data-processing technologies.

The enormous power of communication technologies joined forces with the colossal capacity of the computer for data processing. For example, in 1992, AT&T was transferring information from Chicago to the East Coast at the rate of 6.6 gigabits/second. This meant that the information contained in 1 000 books could travel across the globe each second (Wriston 1992). The spread of data transmission has been increasing in a geometric progression ever since. A more dramatic example is the Kuwaiti bank, which was moved across the national border by fax in 1990, when Iraq occupied the country. The manager of the

---

[5] Hannah Arendt (1906–75), a German–American political theorist, fled the Nazis in 1941. She went to the United States and taught at leading universities. In *The Origins of Totalitarianism* (1951), which established her as a major political thinker, she traced the origins of Nazism and communism to the 19th century.

bank transmitted all of its key documents to its branch in Bahrain at the same time as the Iraqi soldiers were moving into the country: "The next morning the bank opened up as a Bahraini institution neither subject to the freeze on Kuwaiti assets nor to Iraqi control" (Weidenbaum 1994–95, pp. 186–192).

The Internet, this enormous source of power, is accessible to anyone visiting the nearest public library, which enables individuals, as well as groups, to be active players in global politics. The revolt of the masses has truly found an effective channel of expression in the Internet. What is also astonishing is that, together, communication technologies and the hardware of computers have shrunk the limitations of space and time and enabled people to communicate across cultural boundaries, although the reaction to this important process varies from country to country: in some areas of the world, the market economy is growing quickly; in others, civil society and democratization are expanding; and in still others, "illiberal" democracies are emerging.

The human condition at the end of the millennium is thus marked by Ibn Khaldun's sense of a "new creation." This sophisticated phase in human history is conveyed through the overworked and rather obscure term, *globalization*. Globalization is not, as the term suggests, the homogenization of human communities — our diverse identities challenge the notion of any *a priori* body of accepted and objective truth (as would be apparent if the same rules and norms were observed and practiced by everyone) — although globalization has generated a good deal of harmonization in functional areas, such as those of consumer products, financial services, and the production of "values."[6] Common features do bind human beings as one

7

---

[6] Any dynamic and active unit or system produces goods, services, and values. The first two are obvious because they represent the utility of the system in the production of either use or exchange value, or both, but the last one is not as clear. *Value* in this sense refers to the ability of a system or unit to produce symbols, norms, or mores that contribute to the standing, status, and longevity of the system. The production of "value" makes members of a system observe, uphold, and preserve it as something worth more than its utilitarian value. As will be shown, globalization is revealing features of such a system.

species, but each human being is unique. Globalization, moreover, is not a project manipulated by a specific group or state interested in imposing its will and views on others, as the combination of "information revolution" and "revolt of the masses" has removed the possibility of any given player's establishing a monopoly on information. Globalization is therefore best described as a "process," rather than as a "project." No doubt, one can trace the origins of this process to America and further back to Europe, but nothing makes it exclusively American or European. Just because the agrarian revolution originated in Mesopotamia and the industrial revolution first happened in England, this does not mean these revolutions were particularly Middle Eastern or European. Many people, especially those with a weakness for conspiracy theories, suggest that globalization is a new phase of imperialism that emerged initially as interdependence and now as globalization. Even if this claim was at one time plausible, I think it is no longer so, simply because the process of globalization has become so vast and complex.

In this essay, I examine globalization and its dynamics and put these into historical perspective. I follow a dual process capturing the nature of the transformation of the world's condition and setting off a boundary for this new creation to identify its consequences. My principal argument is that mainstream social theories, specifically those in the fields of international relations and world politics, fail to adequately consider the important changes brought by globalization. As Bienenstock and Homer-Dixon (1998, p. A21) recently observed in the *Globe and Mail*, the contemporary world scene "resembles, rather than the closed and predictable mechanism of a clock, something closer to the open and chaotic system of weather." Moreover, mainstream theories rely entirely on the philosophical presuppositions of the Westphalian age — exclusive national interest and the primacy of *raison d'État* (reason of state: placing the needs of the nation above the privileges of its most important groups). I suggest that globalization has begun a new phase

in human civilization based on the "information mode of production." Unlike the industrial mode of production, which created one world of industry based on modernity, this one is apt
to lead to a paradoxical world of "one civilization—many civilizations," a world in which many assumptions are shared, but
each has a variety of manifestations. Although this new world
will envelop the whole of humanity, it will also allow diverse cultures to strike their own balance with and within it. The interaction of the various components of this global civilization will
require a sophisticated understanding, tolerance, and above all
the common celebration of the future, or, as R.B.J. Walker
(1988) suggested, the celebration of "one world, many worlds."
Unlike the industrial civilization, which more or less relied on
the Western narrative of modernity, this one allows for a
"multinarrative," giving rise to one civilization within which
many can flourish.

9

In this book, I hope to present a theoretical framework for
making sense of this volatile post-Cold War situation and provide a practical methodology for global governance. I hope to
define a context to enable constructive dialogue among people
striving to remain unique and distinct in the face of global and,
in some ways, homogenizing interactions. As well, I try to go
beyond the "monoculture mind-set" described by Vandana
Shiva (1993, p. 11), the Indian environmentalist and feminist,
and encourage tolerance and, better still, the celebration of
others. It may appear at times that I have overstepped the
bounds of objective scholarship and scientific inquiry and
entered the rather tricky territory of the prediction, or fore-
casting, of the future. What in reality I have attempted to do is
to combine description and prescription in a time of deep
transformation and theoretical deconstruction and reconstruction. Such a paradoxical combination of scholarship *cum*
prophecy is not new. Any intellectual or writer is responsible
for both the tedious task of accurately describing the present
and that of pointing out trends to help in understanding and
shaping the future, tasks that together entail the guardianship of

tradition and the "vanguardship" of the future (Rajaee 1994).[7] Observations of the new world, or the new creation, in this phase of human civilization are no exception. Talk of a new phase implies new ways of seeing and doing. Any new paradigm or theory developed in the attempt to understand it has to come to grips with relations of theory and practice, or knowledge and power, as they manifest themselves at the close of this century, and this millennium. Globalization has inaugurated a new phase in the copenetration of theory and practice, knowledge and power (Darby 1998a, b). This point will be further elaborated on in the concluding chapter.

What would be the most proper way to understand globalization and this new creation? Are we to continue to operate according to the "conflict model" so readily accepted and dominant in the West, or are we to adopt the "cooperative model," as people of vision have hoped? Will civilizations in the age of the global village interact and borrow and profit from one another, as they have mostly done throughout history, or will they clash, as has been suggested they must? How can one appreciate the "other" in an age in which humanity as a whole is alienated from itself and all human beings have become "others"? What is the relevance of past civilizations? These are some of the questions that guide the discussion in this book.

APPROACH AND METHOD

In explaining the human condition today, Ernest Gellner maintained, in *Postmodernism, Reason and Religion* (1992, p. 1), that "there are three fundamental and irreducible positions. Three primary colours are required for mapping our condition." As the title of Gellner's book suggests, these primary positions are the following (Gellner 1992, p. vii):

---

[7] The paradoxical nature of the "guardian *cum* vanguard" is very important, because if tradition is not respected the result will be uprooting and alienating, whereas if there is no "vanguarding" of change, the end result will be stagnation and lack of progress.

-❦ Postmodernism, or "relativism, in a variety of formulations, which forswears the idea of a unique truth, but tries to treat each particular vision as if it were none the less true";

-❦ Utilitarian rationalism (Gellner's own position), which "retains the faith in the uniqueness of truth, but does not believe we ever possess it definitively"; and

-❦ "Fundamentalism, which believes in a unique truth and which believes itself to be in possession of it."

Moreover, Gellner (1992, p. 1) added,

> It would be quite wrong to try to reduce any one of them to a mere extreme exaggeration or modification of any one of the others, or to see it as a compromise version of the two others. Each expresses a fundamental option of the human spirit, when facing the world as it is now.

Gellner's work leaves us with the impression that these three positions are so far apart that they represent three distinct ways of being human. In reality, each position simply reflects one component of what makes us human. To assign rationality to certain groups only and cast others as traditionalists or irrationalists ignores the most fundamental aspect of human beings, who are rational by nature. I think rationality flows like blood within us, except that, depending on the time and place, it takes different forms.

What Gellner called "rationalism" is only one form of rationality, that is, utilitarian rationality, supported by either experimental verification or utility. This form of rationality lies at the heart of Western modernity. As argued by the fathers of utilitarianism, Jeremy Bentham (1748–1832) and John Stuart Mill (1806–73), it supports an order that benefits as many people as possible and harms as few as possible (Scarre 1996). Mill, in 1861, defined utilitarianism as follows:

> The creed which accepts as the foundation of morals, "Utility," or the "Greatest Happiness Principle," holds that actions are right in proportion as they tend to promote happiness, wrong as they tend to produce the reverse of happiness. By happiness is intended pleasure,

and the absence of pain; by unhappiness, pain, and the privation of
pleasure.

— Mill (1949, chap. 2)

Rationality may also take a normative form and help people ascertain some form of ethical certainty. Otherwise, one has to accept the assertion that religious-minded people and those who try to live by the standards of their religious beliefs are irrational. But can this be said of St Augustine (354–430), the Christian thinker, or Abu al-Nasr Al-Farabi (870–950), the founder of Islamic philosophy, or St Thomas Aquinas (d. 1274), and the like? Certainly, they were rational. Religious-minded people employ a rationality, too, but they invoke it in a different form. They follow what may be called "moral rationality," that is, a rationality that defines its categories on the basis of right and wrong or vice and virtue and bases its validity on textual and hermeneutic comprehension.

Finally, can one deny rationality to the contemplative minds of those who question, criticize, and investigate our existence? Do we not revere Rene Descartes for his famous axiom, "I think, therefore, I am," and aspire to fulfill Marx's dictum that the aim of knowledge and philosophy is to change things? Again, I think that we do so aspire, and I feel that in doing so we propagate "positive," or scientific, rationality and thereby enhance emancipation.

As will be elaborated on in the next chapter, the multiple nature of humanity generates various kinds of rationality, each catering to a particular human need. Abraham Harold Maslow's much-talked-about concept of a "hierarchy of needs" suggests that humanity begins with basic physical needs, then moves all the way up to the need for "self actualization" (Maslow 1970).[8]

---

[8] A humanistic psychologist, Maslow set up a hierarchy of needs in which all the basic needs are at the bottom and those concerning humanity's highest potential are at the top. The hierarchical theory is often represented as a pyramid, with the larger, lower levels representing the lower needs and the apex representing the need for self-actualization. Each level of the pyramid depends on the previous level. He had five categories of needs: physiological needs; needs for safety, or security; those for love, affection, and the sense of belonging; those for esteem and self-respect; and the need for self-actualization.

Although these needs form an interesting pyramid, I feel they are more interrelated than hierarchical and that they all stem from one overarching need for security, which has three components: moral serenity, certainty, and worldly satisfaction. Moral rationality helps generate a feeling of serenity and balance; scientific, or positive, rationality provides a sense of meaning, certainty, and predictability; and utilitarian rationality facilitates the satisfaction of various needs and desires. The moment people come to form communal life and, particularly, the highest form of such life — a civilization — they require a balanced mix of all three. A successful civilization needs each type of rationality to manifest itself and play its proper role.

I feel that in practice the prevalent approaches to the study of the human condition rather faithfully accept Gellner's classification of his three approaches to reasoning. Obviously, an extremist group promoting particular, parochial, and exclusive interests can easily adopt any one of these one-sided positions. Such people propagate a Manichean world view, appeal to radical populism, and project a binary world divided in terms of "us" and "them." Paradoxically, extremism and radical populism are on the rise at a critical juncture in human history, when the world is getting smaller and people live in what the Greeks used to call the *oikoumene* (one inhabited quarter). Despite the fact that the overwhelming events of recent decades have intensified this experience of living in a global "life world," our understanding, tolerance, and appreciation of one another have actually decreased. Two of the events listed above exacerbate the problem while presenting opportunities to solve it. First, the fall of the Soviet empire destroyed the bipolar world order and undermined many of the familiar rules of the game in the international arena. Second, the information revolution has opened up new horizons and a new arena requiring new rules of the game.

The mainstream social theories view the human condition compartmentally, with each such theory concentrating exclusively on politics, economics, society, or culture, whereas in the

13

words of Mircea Eliade a "holistic system of knowledge — integrating the scientific, philosophic, religious, and artistic approaches and creation — might become again possible in the future."[9] Given the civilizational nature of the globalization process and the opportunities at hand, this possibility has to be turned into a requirement. Globalization has enabled horizontal linkages among the various spheres of human activity. It no longer makes sense to distinguish high and low politics, although it used to be a truism that issues of security and political instability enjoyed higher priority and belonged to high politics and that economic and social issues had lower priority and belonged to low politics. Although many people now reverse the order of priority, a growing number endorse a multidisciplinary approach to dealing with issues in the public domain. Thus, I adopt the approach in which rationality takes a variety of forms — the normative, the positive, and the utilitarian — and these forms of rationality are logically interlinked.

Gellner's distinction should be recognized, but the way Gellner portrays his three modes of reasoning would make them inevitably lead to what I have termed a "battle of worldviews" (Rajaee 1997, pp. 3–4) and a zero-sum game; indeed, the result would be what Samuel Huntington (1993) has termed a "clash of civilizations." I feel that the various ways people reason differ more in degree than in kind. It may even be possible to establish a division of labour. A distinction of degree among forms of rationality would be conducive to forming an arena in which a "battle of ideas" would flourish and the dialectical interaction of ideas would lead to intellectual growth. The distinction between the "battle of ideas" and the "battle of worldviews" is important because the former leads to a flourishing of ideas and intellectual growth, whereas the latter leads to a zero-sum game in which the proponents of differing worldviews feel they need to eliminate one another (Rajaee 1997). In a battle of

---

[9] From a speech entitled, "Waiting for the Dawn," delivered 26 Oct 1982 (quoted in Carrasco and Swanberg 1985, p. iii).

ideas, diverse modes of reasoning differ as contraries, whereas in a battle of worldviews, they differ as contradictories:

> Contraries pose sharp differences, for example, between plants and animals, men and women, Americans and Canadians, students and teachers, but they never allow the contrast to exclude the possibility of rapprochement and even, from time to time, inversion. Contradictories, however, are incommensurate opposite.
> — Lawrence (1989, p. 17)

The "holistic approach" regards the three forms of rationality outlined above as contraries, definitely not as contradictories. When these forms of rationality function concomitantly, the end result is a dynamic civilization, as will be shown in the next chapter.

The holistic approach takes civilization as its unit of study. Accordingly, during the age of the industrial civilization, based on modernity, the territorial and sovereignty-bound state was the prevalent unit of political organization. But it seems to have lost its importance. What new form the polity takes will depend on its emerging civilizational underpinnings. Polity, as Ibn Khaldun explained, has the

> same relationship to civilization as form has to matter. (The form) is the shape that preserves the existence of (matter) through the (particular) kind (of phenomenon) it represents. It has been established in philosophy that the one cannot be separated from the other. One cannot imagine a dynasty [political order] without a civilization.
> — Ibn Khaldun (1958, vol. 2, p. 300)

Civilization is a broad framework. It includes not only traditional factors — such as political institutions, military power, and cultural mores — but also the more contemporary social factors, such as ecology, economy, and patterns of communal life.

A "civilizational approach" also influences the method of research. The most appropriate method is interdisciplinary. A distinction is drawn in this work between the theoretical approach used to formulate propositions and hypotheses and the practical method used to juxtapose ideas and findings. My theoretical approach is "complex integrative," integrating the

15

three forms of rationality and thereby accounting for the dialectical interaction of the various theories developed in the discourse. My practical method is the procedure that Edward Osborne Wilson, the biologist, Pulitzer Prize winner, Crawford Prize winner, and "father" of sociobiology, called "consilience," or the harmonization of data and analyses from different lines of inquiry (Wilson 1998). Wilson called for the consilience of the natural and social sciences to equip humanity with the analytical and predictive capacity to meet the many challenges ahead. This complex, holistic approach is interdisciplinary, drawing on scholarly achievements in the humanities and the natural and social sciences. Contributions from the arts, anthropology, communications, economics, history, international relations, philosophy, political science and theory, and sociology are all particularly important to understanding the human condition.

This comprehensive approach avoids the reductionist tendency of theories relying on a single cause to explain all social phenomena, as well as avoiding the one-dimensional purpose of theorizing that aims for socialization and conformity. Instead, it embraces all aspects of our paradoxical condition and identifies opportunities for bridging and interacting, rather than for separating and distinguishing. Edward Said, literary theorist and professor of literature at Columbia University, described how the great early-20th-century French poet Paul Valéry (1871–1945) praised Leonardo da Vinci (1452–1519) for his ultimate faith in the human ability to go one step farther:

> *Valéry says that the Italian artist could not but think of a bridge whenever he thought of an abyss. Metaphorically speaking, an abyss is the equivalent of what is presented to us as immutable, definitive, impossible to go beyond. No matter how deep and problematic the scene that presented itself to him, Leonardo always had the capacity to think of some alternative to it, some way of solving the problem, some gift for not passively accepting what was given to him, as if the scene that Leonardo imagined could always be envisioned in a different, and perhaps more hopeful, way.*
>
> — Said (1998, p. 4)

Here, I hope to follow Leonardo's example and explore the possibility of building bridges and connections and show that globalization might be providing the intellectual opportunity and raw material for such an endeavour. History has shown that it is easy to formulate an exclusivist framework for the future but much harder to create a participatory context in which everyone feels accepted and welcome. I venture to say that globalization has given us such an opportunity, provided we make proper use of it. The next chapter explores the main features of this opportunity.

A Theory of Globalization

Labeling is the first act of description
yet, all labels may be liable.

— John Sigler[10]

The dawn of globalization is in sight, and speculation about its nature and direction dominates public discourse. What form of international order is globalization inaugurating? Has it generated a "New World Order," as declared by American President George Bush on 11 September 1990, before a joint session of the Congress of the United States (Bush 1991, vol. II, p. 1222)? Is globalization an economic phenomenon, restructuring the world's economic system from within, as in the view that currently seems prevalent in the field of international political economy? Is it the burgeoning culture of a new era? Is it just the old world of power politics writ large, on a global scale? An honest response to each of these questions would be "no one knows." The closest one can come to giving an answer to any of them would be to suggest that it may be the beginning of a new world order and, even more accurately, an opening up of a range of new opportunities (stemming from globalization). Like any other major historical development, this new phase has

---

[10] I have heard Professor Sigler repeat this theme in his lectures and warn his audience against falling into the trap of the absolutism of concepts.

presented humanity with a *tabula rasa*, and both those in the scholarly and elite community and those in the popular mass media are pondering the meaning and future of globalization.

Competition occurs among paradigms to explain this phenomenon and the future shape of our globalized world. In this process, one can identify two distinct trends. One is to completely dismiss globalization as another phase in the life of "imperialism," a new conspiracy, with the end result that the rich will get richer and the poor will get poorer. Still, it claims that it has an alternative paradigm, based on a religious framework. Another trend is to look at globalization with an inquisitive eye and try to make sense of it. The traditional Western compartmentalization of human life into four areas — politics, economics, culture, and religion — has given rise to four possible paradigms. A review of these paradigms is in order, before I embark on an explanation of my complex alternative theory.

POLITICAL APPROACH, THE END OF CIVILITY

In the aftermath of the French Revolution, Immanuel Kant proposed his plan for a "perpetual peace," claiming that in a world of liberal states there would be no war. After the collapse of the Soviet empire and the punishment of Saddam Hussein for invading Kuwait, President George Bush addressed, in October 1990, the 45th session of the United Nations General Assembly in a similar vein:

> *I see a world of open borders, open trade and most importantly, open minds; a world that celebrates the common heritage that belongs to all the world's people, taking pride not just in hometown or homeland but in humanity itself. I see a world touched by a spirit, that of the Olympics, based not on competition that's driven by fear but sought out of joy and exhilaration and a true quest for excellence. And I see a world where democracy continues to win new friends and convert old foes and where the Americas — North, Central, and South — can provide a model for the future of all humankind: the world's first completely democratic hemisphere. And I see a world building on the*

emerging new model of European unity, not just Europe but the whole world and free.

— Bush (1991, vol. II, p. 1332)

This was the optimistic mood in the United States after the previous president, Ronald Reagan, the 40th American president (in office 1981–89), successfully transformed the American failure in Viet Nam into a historical epoch of patriotism and portrayed the Russian defeat in Afghanistan as an American victory. Euphoria was running high. But more importantly, questions concerning the nature of the change turned overnight into a topic of national and international debate. A diplomatic correspondent from the United Kingdom and astute observer, Robert Fisk, characterized this change very well when he said "the American view of the world becomes sacrosanct by satellite" (Fisk 1997). This state of mind portrayed a world of neoliberal economics and the politics of civil society.

21

Originally, the debate about the nature of this change echoed Daniel Bell's (1966) celebrated work *The End of Ideology*. Bell thought then that the success of post-World War II reconstruction, the coming of postindustrial societies, the growth of the white-collar class, the spread of suburbia, and the emergence of behavioural social science, with its language of hypotheses, parameters, variables, and paradigms, indicated the coming of a new era. Nazism, fascism, and "the left" had either failed or proven ineffective. The era of "the end of ideology" had arrived. In Bell's words, this new era "closes the book, intellectually speaking, on an era, the one of easy 'left' formulae for social change" (Bell 1966, p. 405).

Similarly, it was assumed that the end of the Cold War also ended an era. Francis Fukuyama characterized this optimism in his much-debated essay, "The End of History" (Fukuyama 1989). He argued that capitalism and liberal–pluralist politics had triumphed over the dialectic of history, putting an end to history itself. In this state, we were witnessing "the universalization of Western liberal democracy as the final form of human government" (Fukuyama 1989, p. 4). Later, in a book with a similar title, *The End of History and the Last Man*, Fukuyama argued that Western liberal democracy was going to be the ultimate faith of humanity as a whole: "There is a fundamental process at work that dictates a common evolutionary pattern for *all* human societies — in short, something like a Universal History of mankind in the direction of liberal democracy" (Fukuyama 1992, p. 48, emphasis in the original).

But this optimistic paradigm was short lived. In its place has emerged a pessimistic one, expressed best in the phrase "the end of civility." Robert D. Kaplan, Samuel Huntington, and Farid Zakaria have developed this paradigm. Globalization has, accordingly, enveloped everybody and made a player of those who were formerly unable to voice their concerns. Zakaria argued that this has given rise to many polities that are democratic insofar as they employ democratic processes and institutions but that fail to share the underlying value system that guarantees human rights and the freedom of the individual. He began his essay, "The Rise of Illiberal Democracy," with the following observation:

> The American diplomat Richard Holbrooke pondered a problem on the eve of the September 1996 elections in Bosnia, which were meant to restore civic life to that ravaged country. "Suppose the election was declared free and fair," he said, and those elected are "racists, fascists, separatists, who are publicly opposed to [peace and reintegration]. This is the dilemma."
>
> — Zakaria (1997, p. 22)

Globalization has enabled mob politics, as populist democracies have replaced pluralistic ones. Illiberal populist democracies place no limits on the powers that be and have no respect for constitutional privileges or constraints, such as the rule of law, private-property rights, separation of powers, free speech, and freedom of assembly.

More directly related to this discussion is a notion expressed in Kaplan's (1994) article, "The Coming of Anarchy." Kaplan described a scenario in which the existing order had collapsed into environmental crises and massive movement of populations. Globalization had divided humanity into a privileged class of people that *Le Monde* had termed a "cosmocracy" (who were boarding planes bound for Seoul, Hong Kong, Singapore, and Tokyo) and a marginalized class of downtrodden souls. For Kaplan, the breakdown of the Westphalian state system, where "war-making entities will no longer be restricted to a specific territory," has become the name of the game. A definition of the good in terms of the national interest has given way to parochial tribalism, and in the process "technology will be used toward primitive ends" (Kaplan 1994, p. 73). Kaplan described these two worlds as follows:

> *We are entering a bifurcated world. Part of the globe is inhabited by Hegel's and Fukuyama's Last Man, healthy, well fed, and pampered by technology. The other, larger, part is inhabited by Hobbes's First Man, condemned to a life that is "poor, nasty, brutish, and short." Although both parts will be threatened by environmental stress, the Last Man will be able to master it; the First Man will not.*
> — Kaplan (1994, p. 60)

23

A yet more pessimistic view was presented by Huntington (1993, 1996) under the rubric of "the clash of civilizations." He claimed that he was presenting a new paradigm to explain "the emerging pattern of conflict and cooperation on the global scene after the Cold War" (Huntington 1997a, p. 141). Like Kaplan, Huntington claimed that the state system had lost most of its authority, and in response to the question of where power and authority would and should lie in the world, Huntington felt that culture and civilization had become the proper entities for political loyalty: "The world is in some sense two, but the central distinction is between the West as the hitherto dominant civilization and all others" (Huntington 1996, p. 36). Huntington identified eight civilizations — Chinese, Japanese, Indian, Islamic, Western, Orthodox Russian, Latin American, and possibly African — as dominant forces in world politics.[11] *Raison d'État* in

---

[11] In his *Foreign Affairs* article, he used the term *Confucian* for *Chinese*. But in his book, he argued that the former is a major component of the latter and that Chinese civilization "appropriately describes the common culture of China and the Chinese communities in Southeast Asia and elsewhere outside China as well as the related cultures of Vietnam and Korea" (Huntington 1996, p. 45).

the state system was defined in terms of material interests, and compromise and balance of interests and power were possibilities, although in this system culture and civilization were related to a world of values in which compromise was difficult, if not impossible. Globalization in the post-Cold War era denotes merely a phase of the ongoing clash of civilizations, one in which interests are defined by ethnic and religious identities. However, Huntington's political paradigm explains only one aspect of humanity's life world, that of competition, whereas there is more to life than competition and struggle.

ECONOMIC APPROACH, THE END OF GEOGRAPHY

The most prevalent view of globalization is that of economists who see it in terms of increased economic interdependence and the integration of all national economies into one economy within the framework of a capitalist market. To paraphrase Lenin, at the most advanced stage of capitalism, capital dictates the norms and sets the social agenda. The proponents of this view celebrate the ultimate triumph of the Western capitalist system and claim that "free marketers" have won over the "social engineers." The global market, not ideologies or political actors, determines the future. This new system began to emerge even before the destruction of political bipolarity. For example, Peter Drucker argued in 1986 that the world economy had been transformed. "The talk today is of the 'changing world economy'. I wish to argue that the world economy is not 'changing'; it has already changed — in its foundations and its structure — and in all probability the change is irreversible" (Drucker 1986, p. 768). The most important aspect of this change entails a shift in commodities, from capital and materials to knowledge. The prices of raw materials have collapsed. Take petroleum as one example — its current price is one-fifth of what it was in 1979. However, in terms of efficiency, the world has advanced remarkably. "In 1984, for every unit of industrial production, Japan consumed only 60 percent of raw material consumed for the same volume of industrial material production in 1973, 11 years earlier" (Drucker 1986, p. 773).

A drastic change in the mode of production has occurred: from industry to information technology. We have left the age of Fordism for that of post-Fordism. Whereas the Fordist economy was localized inside certain national borders and the assembly line of a big plant or factory, the post-Fordist considers economic nationalism an impediment to production and replaces assembly lines with a decentralized and geographically scattered process of "production sharing." A division of labour between polities with technical know-how and those with cheap raw materials and labour gave rise to the notion of "comparative advantage," an advantage based on consumer demand and the availability of markets. Production sharing based on technical and political comparative advantage has made Singapore the biggest producer of computer hardware and Bangladesh the biggest producer of men's clothing.

These changes signify the emergence of a global market. In addition, the power of computer communications technologies has changed the nature of finance and trade, thus putting an end to geography, creating a borderless world, and signaling the twilight of sovereignty (O'Brien 1992). In this new phase, nation-states no longer play the central role, which is now played by large corporations. In the new global market, "rules no longer apply solely to specific geographical frameworks, such as the nation-state or other typical regulatory jurisdictional territories" (O'Brien 1992, p. 1). This applies not only to the rules of the game but also to such an important institution as property. As O'Brien (1992, p. 100) explained, "ownership is more and more international and global, divorced from national definitions". Hence, sovereign territorial states have lost their relevance, and the age of global governance has begun. The proponents of the theory of international political economy tell us that cooperation among economic institutions will replace politics, as globalization has practically ended competition and established a harmonious global marketplace.

Insightful observers have been warning of the danger of putting too much faith in economic forces and the market. For example, Karl Polanyi, in his now classic work, *The Great Transformation* (1944, p. 73), wrote that "to allow the market mechanism to be the sole director of the fate of human beings and their natural environment, indeed, even of the amount and use of purchasing power, would result in demolition of society." The reported success of free-market economics has blinded many people. For a decade, the market triumphed, and everyone was impressed with the Asian miracle, where production went side by side with development. However, an important component of economic development was ignored, namely, the middle class, which Ralf Dahrendorf (1959) recognized as the backbone of modern bourgeois society. As well, the Asian countries gave birth to an immature market, without the supporting social infrastructure.

It is interesting to note that the proponents of the economic approach reacted as strongly to the negative backlash of globalization in the late 1990s, when the market demonstrated the one-sided nature of the Asian miracle. As reported by the CBC, the international financier and philanthropist, George Soros (*b.* 1930 in Budapest) declared, in October 1998, that "global capitalism was coming apart" and that the world was facing its worst economic crisis in half a century. People like Robert Reich (1992), the former US Secretary of Labor, warned that the problem was more political than economic, but their warnings fell on deaf ears.

CULTURAL APPROACH, THE END OF OBJECTIVITY

The third response to the challenge of the new creation is rather critical. It argues that Karl Marx predicted the coming of this new world in, for example, the following passage from *The Communist Manifesto*:

> *All fixed fast-frozen relations, with their train of ancient venerable prejudices and opinions are swept away, all newly formed ones become*

antiquated before they can ossify. All that is solid melts into air, all that is holy is profaned, and man is at last compelled to face with sober senses, his real conditions of life, and his relations with his kind. The need of constantly expanding market for its products chases the bourgeoisie over the whole surface of the globe. It must nestle everywhere, settle everywhere, and establish connections everywhere.

          — Marx and Engels (1973, p. 83)

This "melting into air" has so affected our philosophical and cultural understanding that the old paradigms no longer explain what is going on.

Culture, as defined by prominent anthropologist Clifford Geertz (1973, p. 89), "denotes a historically transmitted pattern of meanings embodied in symbols, a system of inherited conceptions expressed in symbolic forms." Culture not only helps us define ourselves but also is the means by "which men communicate, perpetuate, and develop their knowledge about and attitudes towards life." But which "pattern of meanings" should we accept in a world of many cultures? All existing patterns of meaning have lost their relevance. Indeed, long before the coming of the information age, the philosopher Karl Jaspers suggested that what the world desperately needed was a universal philosophy. In an autobiographical essay, he wrote that "we are on the road from the evening-glow of European philosophy to the dawn of world philosophy" (1957, pp. 83–84).

The familiar sociocultural paradigms were communism and democratic capitalism, both of which constituted and projected alternative forms of modernity. Globalization has crystallized the crisis of modernity as a paradigm, and the alternative paradigm has been dubbed "postmodernity," which can be said to have one important objective, the "deconstruction" of former paradigms and theories; indeed, Bernstein called postmodernism "a rage against humanism and the Enlightenment legacy" (1985, p. 25). Underlying that rage is the conviction that the existing paradigms are but "constructions" of one kind or another, intended to serve particular interests (Harvey 1990). This conviction echoes certain remarks of Nietzsche, who declared at the end of the last century that "we know no fact independent of interpretation; there is no vision of reality untainted by prejudice and perspective" (cited in Lawrence 1989, p. 90). Postmodernism rejects the modernist ideals of rationality, "virility" (as what has a masculine spirit), artistic genius, and individualism in favour of anticapitalism, contempt for traditional morality, and commitment to radical egalitarianism. Philosophy professor Jean-François Lyotard defined the postmodern condition as "incredulity toward metanarratives."[12] Unlike the project of modernity, which involves a belief in the metanarrative of objective reality, verifiable by experience, postmodernity brands all held truth as construction. This postmodern way of thinking differs from both modern and premodern thought. Table 1 gives the general characteristics of the three ways of understanding the human condition, which are the three important phases of humanity's civilizational saga. The comparison may help to clarify the claims of postmodernism. Schematic differences appear among the ways each epoch views itself, defines its *telos*, and formulates its patterns, its modes of thinking, and its icons.

Premodern, *modern*, and *postmodern* are of course labels to explain and help us understand some broad trends, but one should note that they are uncertain and equivocal. Some features are shared by each of the three epochs, and some features overlap. Both premodern and modern ways of thinking convey certainty: the certainty of premodernism is based on the centrality of the gods or God, whereas that of modernism is based on science. Postmodernist thought denies any ground for thinking in terms of a definite theological or scientifically verifiable system. Both the premodern and postmodern ways of thinking invite one to appreciate the totality of existence, the former out of religious conviction and the latter out of the realization that our Earth is precarious and requires our care.

---

[12]   This is from his now famous report for the Province of Quebec's Conseil des universités (council of universities), which he prepared in 1979. See Lyotard (1984).

Table 1. The main features of premodern, modern, and postmodern thought.

Premodern	Modern	Postmodern
Nomos	*Logos*	Icon
Naturalism	Romanticism or symbolism	Paraphysics or dadaism
Ideals	Form (conjunctive, closed)	Antiform (disjunctive, open)
Purpose	Purpose	Play
Ordinance	Design	Chance
Hierarchy	Hierarchy	Anarchy
Discovery, revelation	Construction, totalization	Deconstruction, rediscovery
Thesis	Antithesis	Synthesis
Text	Boundary	Intertext
Communal truth	Paradigm	Regimes of truths
Interpretation	Interpretation	Variety of interpretations
Immanence	Transcendence	Immanence

Source: The author developed this table partly from Hassan (1985), who laid out a dichotomous table to show the difference between modernism and postmodernism.

Thus, postmodernism aims to emancipate humanity from itself by making it conscious of its shortcomings. Globalization has shown us that our subjective paradigms have shaped our understanding of the world and the people around us. We are told, in the words of postmodernist theorist Michel Foucault (1972, 1973), that a strong "archeology of knowledge" is required to deconstruct the existing paradigms. Using critical theory as the new methodological mechanism, postmodernism has produced feminist, identity, green, environmental, downtrodden, ethnic, religious, and class theories and politics. The most recent feature of postmodernism is the rise of political correctness and the attempt to purge dissenting opinion from the ranks of the academic—artistic—professional caste, together with a systematic attack on excellence in all fields. Postmodernism has become an anti-Enlightenment position; its adherents believe that what went before, that is, modernism, depended inappropriately on reason, rationalism, and wisdom and was inherently elitist and nonmulticultural, therefore oppressive. As a result, the proponents of these new schools of thought declare the end of objective reality and insist that the world and our understanding of it are subjective, the construction of various group or class interests, in short, a mere narrative.

At face value, this means anybody's understanding is as valid as anybody else's, and this in turn leads to a world in which we have no common ground for either communication or practical cooperation. Here lies an interesting dilemma. No doubt globalization has removed physical barriers in the way of cultural interaction. But as more and more people get involved in more than one culture, practical problems of intercultural communication increase (Featherstone 1990). Reverting to absolute relativism only aggravates the situation.

RELIGIOUS AND SECULAR RADICAL APPROACH, THE END OF INQUIRY

The fourth response to the new world comes from radical-minded individuals and groups of both religious and secular kinds who have also taken a position vis-à-vis globalization. Globalization cuts across all religious traditions. For many of these traditions, the world has not changed; rather, a new form of the old divide between the righteous and the deviant or, in the language of more revolutionary types, the oppressors and the oppressed has become fashionable. Similarly, for the radical Marxists globalization has sharpened the old divide between the oppressors and the oppressed.

The prominent Islamic scholar, Mahmoud Ayoub, defined globalization in the following way: "It is said that we now live in a global village. To extent that it is true, it is a negative process. Globalization is the latest manifestation of Western imperialism" (Ayoub 1999, session 1, Friday morning, 9 Apr). This is simply a recent echo of a bigger movement. Since the 1970s a powerful trend has emerged under the rubric of religious fundamentalism. Ironically, despite its apparent propagation of a return to traditional religion, it is neither conservative nor "traditionalist," in the sense of preserving the status quo of a revived past. Instead, this new fundamentalism is radical, modern, and in many cases revolutionary. It presents a paradigm for understanding the human condition in all its contexts, including globalization. The proponents of this approach believe that they own the truth and that their way of presenting it is the only way, not only for their own coreligionists but also for humanity as a whole.

Two of the most famous protagonists of religious fundamentalism in recent decades were the leader of the 1979 Islamic revolution, Ayatollah Khomeini, and the most articulate ideological leader of the Islamic movement in the Arab world, Seyyed Qutb (executed 1966). Both saw the ultimate solution to all problems in their way of understanding Islam, and both saw the world in binary opposition of "us" and "them." Khomeini termed the poles of this opposition the "oppressors" (*mostakbaran*) and the "oppressed" (*mostaz'afan*), and Qutb termed them "ignorance" (*jahiliyya*) and "Islam."[13] They considered those parts of the world not ruled under the Islamic system — and here we can include areas not ruled under "religious codes of conduct" — the realms of ignorance and oppression, even though individuals in these areas may confess to and live by God's commandments. To paraphrase Qutb, a society whose legislation is not based on divine law is improper, however much its individuals may proclaim themselves religious (Kepel 1985).

Obviously, globalization falls into Qutb's category of ignorance, and he thought it was up to the people of God "to establish the reign of God on Earth and eliminate the reign of man" (from Qutb's controversial book, *The Signpost*, cited in Kepel 1985, p. 55). This approach is expressed in many attempts by more conservative and religious regimes in the Muslim world to restrict the expansion of the Internet. However, sometimes this anger is expressed in jargon reminding one of Marxist and "Third Worldist" vocabularies. The self-righteousness of people who claim we are all under God's judgment differs from that of people who think that God is always on their side. It seems that the new fundamentalism applies to the new global scene, as in the

---

[13]   A comprehensive treatment of Qutb's ideas is found in Moussalli (1992).

following passage from the official organ of the Islamic Youth Movement in Malaysia (Angkatan Belia Islem, Malaysia):

> *"Globalization" is showing itself to be "gobblisation" whereby the dominant western economies might well swallow all of us, ending forever the myth of national sovereignty and ridiculing the struggle of all Third World peoples to be the determiners of their own lives. If "one world" is the coming reality, it must be a peoples' world and not a world of masters and slaves.*
>
> — Gordon and Ali (1998, letter to the editor)

Similarly, for radical Marxists, globalization is a new form of colonization. The journal *Race and Class* devoted a recent issue to "the threat of globalism" (RAC 1998–99). In the view of its authors, information has replaced the gold standard, but exploitation continues. The technological revolution has simply made exploitation a global phenomenon. Radical Marxist writers recognize that the epochal changes of globalization have weakened national borders but conclude that capitalism has been the biggest winner. It is no longer bound by national sovereignty, and thus it has created one world market. Further, the information revolution has made capitalism much more powerful. Now capitalism has enhanced its capacity for production, increased its speed of distribution, and attracted more consumers, using the new communication technologies. As a result, capitalism has integrated world production, markets, finance, culture, and politics, to the point that it is more than a mode of economic production — it is a mode of life. As Sivanandan, the political activist, writer, and founding editor of *Race and Class*, wrote, "If imperialism is the latest stage of capitalism, globalism is the latest stage of imperialism" (RAC 1998–99, p. 5).

CRITIQUE OF THESE PARADIGMS

A quest for an understanding of the human condition is only possible with open-minded philosophical inquiry, that is, with the art of loving wisdom and truth. Any approach that claims to have already found the truth about anything is bound to reduce reality to dogma, ideology, propaganda, or sophistry. Although it seems that the approaches outlined above operate within the margin of genuine inquiry and partisan positions, I can identify two major problems with them.

The first and most important critical observation one can make about these paradigms is that they are exclusionary and one dimensional. Humanity is seen as only "political" (that is, domineering), economic, cultural, or religious. The secular approaches excessively emphasize utilitarian rationality and ignore religious experience completely,[14] and the religious approach ignores and undermines secular needs and demands. Mary Jo Leddy, a theology professor at the University of Toronto, observed that humanity has a deep hunger for spirituality: "The 19th century was an era of sexual repression, and the 20th century is a time of spiritual repression" (cited in Johnson 1999 [in an interview]). Others have pointed to the religious fundamentalism of the past two decades and felt that too much religiosity has put secularism in a defensive mode and has endangered many human achievements of the past (Burger 1996).

The poverty of "the scientific man" has been well shown and criticized (Morgenthau 1946; Voegelin 1952), and there is no need to repeat this criticism here. Suffice it to say that as a result of this poverty, each approach concentrates on its own disciplinary angle and either ignores other aspects of the issue altogether or subordinates them in a hierarchy of knowledge. One should take multiplicity as integral to the human condition, using a sophisticated, integrative, interactive approach. The mundane manifestation of human desires, aptitudes, and actualizations is multilayered: human beings are simultaneously political, economic, cultural, and religious. (This matter will be addressed more comprehensively when I present my alternative, more complex theory.)

33

---

[14] Eric Voegelin spent all his professional life showing that political order is directly related to religious experience. A collection of essays (Hughes 1999) elaborates on this notion.

A revealing article by Robert Samuelson (1998) captured this crucial shortcoming of contemporary science. Commenting on Federal Reserve Chairman Alan Greenspan's report to the US Congress on the Asian crisis, Samuelson stated that despite all the data and the deductive theories available, neither he nor Greenspan knew what was going on. The source of their confusion lay in the seductive power of compartmentalized theories and disciplines that failed to account for the complex relationship between politics and culture. Nor did they account for C.P. Snow's (1959) critical observation regarding the prevailing distinction between two cultures, one "scientific," the other "human." Snow felt that instead of this sharp division between scientists and intellectuals, one should aim at educating people who will be "trained not only in scientific but in human terms" (Snow 1959, p. 45).

My second criticism of the approaches outlined above concerns "the internal logic"[15] of the four paradigms. I feel that despite their obvious differences, they each make one important common claim, namely, that globalization has eroded politics as hitherto known in human history. All fit a framework that may be called the "end-of-politics" paradigm — which is extreme, if not dangerous. Aristotle's notion that human beings are political by nature holds true regardless of any other claim about human nature. Politics is a confusing realm of paradoxes simultaneously involving cooperation, competition, conflict management, administration, authoritative allocation of values, dialogue, and clash. Ironically, the proponents of the end of politics preach one thing but practice another, advocating the end of politics but recommending a politics of exclusion, which is unhelpful to the very civilizational milieu they are promoting.

The four approaches follow their own particular interests and concerns. Only people who follow the rule of democracy, the market, special interests (class, gender, or environment), or the

---

[15] Abraham Kaplan has distinguished between "internal" and "reconstructed" logic in the following way: "The logic in use refers to cognition directed to understand the subject matter under study, whereas reconstructed logic is 'in effect a hypothesis'. The usefulness of the latter is in illuminating the logic-in-use of the subject under study rather than presenting a picture which is self serving but removed from the truth" (Kaplan 1964, p. 8).

34

divine path exclusively defined, they seem to say, should have the privilege and opportunity of being actors in the new global village. Even Huntington, who employs the language of civilization, seems to use it as a disguise for the practices of empire. He claims that he does not advocate empire, but his theory implies that the future of politics will be a clash between victorious America and the rest of the world that rejects the American way. A conclusion such as this would have several problems, and I shall address the following three:

-🍃 *Ontological problems* — It perpetuates a one-dimensional view of human nature;

-🍃 *Epistemological problems* — It relies too heavily on utilitarian rationality, that is, the behaviourist approach and the scientific approach; and

-🍃 *Phenomenological problems* — It overlooks or mis-perceives the nature of technology and the information revolution.

Inasmuch as the end-of-politics paradigm suggests an ontology of the human condition, it aggrandizes one aspect of the human essence, portraying it only under its political, economic, cultural, or religious dimension or considering one of these dimensions predominant. Humans are admittedly spatial and temporal. The role of each dimension of the human essence depends on space and time, which suggests the will-to-power aspect of human nature. Anyone who concentrates on this competitive aspect of human relations also emphasizes the Hobbesian understanding of human nature and portrays the human species as *Animus dominandi*. As Huntington put it, "it is human to hate. For self-definition and motivation people need enemies: competitors in business, rivals in achievement, opponents in politics" (1996, p. 130). This is an echo of Hobbes, whose important observation in the *Leviathan* is worth repeating here:

> So that in the nature of man, we find three principal causes of quar-rel. First, Competition; Secondly, Diffidence; Thirdly, Glory. The first maketh men invade for Gain; the second for Safety; and the third, for Reputation. The first use Violence, to make themselves Masters of

other mens persons, wives, children, and cattell; the second, to defend
them; the third, for trifles, as a word, a smile, a different opinion, and
any other signs of undervalue, either direct in their Persons, or by
reflexion in their Kindred, their friends, their Nation, their Profession,
or their Name.

— Hobbes (1968 [1651], pp. 185–186)

Although one must not overlook the prominent place of
power and the importance of power relations in human affairs,
one also needs to consider whether the will to dominate has its
roots in our nature or is the result of an unfriendly physical
world and our insecurity in the face of an "immoral society," to
use the terminology of Christian theologian and philosopher,
Reinhold Niebuhr (1932). To paraphrase Jean-Jacques
Rousseau, are we not born free but everywhere in chains? Is the
dominance of the will to power the result of a worldly feeling of
a "security–power dilemma," to use the expression employed by
Kenneth W. Thompson?[16] Or is the dominance of the will to
power attributable to our very essence? These are major questions, and they should not be overlooked. If the human essence
were only a will to power, it would be natural for people to concentrate on their exclusive self-interest and, by extension, the
interests of their polity; moreover, as nationhood is the basis of
the modern and still prevalent polity (that is, the state), national
interest would be central to politics. Moreover, the main objective of a polity would be to preserve its members' life, property,
and freedom. This idea constitutes the foundation of modern
Western civilization, which explains the persistence of a deter-
ministic, unidimensional view of humanity and the notion that
the struggle for power is inevitable.

As history tells, however, the will to power does not constitute human essence. If "it is human to hate," it is also human to
love and to care. The Christian and Muslim *Weltanchauungen*
attribute this to a failure on the part of humanity to uphold

---

[16] I had the good fortune to study with, and work for, Professor Thompson
as his teaching assistant, from 1979 to 1983. He introduced and explained the
idea of the security–power dilemma in his course, and he and his students
debated it in his graduate seminar, "Normative Theories of International
Relations" at the University of Virginia. I discuss this theory in greater detail
below.

God's commandments. Christianity attributes this to original sin, when the first humans rebelled and behaved contrary to God's will. But the Christian outlook also emphasizes the presence in us of the Holy Spirit, which can help free oneself from a preoccupation with power and power politics.

Islam explains this duality by two important stories. According to the first, God created humanity to act as his vicegerent on Earth, clearly indicating the nobility of human beings:

> And when your Lord said to the angels, "I am going to place on Earth a vicegerent," the angels said, "What! Wilt Thou place therein one who will spread evil therein and shed blood, while we celebrate Thy holiness and glory?" He said, "I know what you do not know."
> — The Qur'an (II: 30)

According to the second story, when God offered "the trust" (al-amana, which many interpreters of the Qur'an have translated as "knowledge," "awareness of good and evil," or "freedom of choice") to "the heavens and the Earth, and the mountains," they did not dare to accept this heavy responsibility. When it was offered to man, he accepted it, because, in God's words, he is "transgressing and ignorant" (the Qur'an, XXXIII: 72). It is this ignorance that made it possible for Satan to deceive both Adam and Eve so that they would approach the forbidden tree. "But Satan made them both fall from it [the heaven], and caused them to depart from the state in which they were" (the Qur'an, II: 36).[17]

In both Christianity and Islam, Adam committed an error and took on the heavy burden of knowledge and the moral dilemma of right and wrong. In the Christian narrative, he ate

37

---

[17] The idea that Satan has such a power over humans has an interesting origin in Islamic religion. After creating a man out of clay, God ordered all angels to prostrate themselves before this new creature. Satan objected and said to God that he was superior. God became angry and asked Satan to leave his presence. Satan then asked God to allow him to have access to Adam as a reward for his many years of service to God but also as a way of proving to God that the human race is inferior, owing to its being unable to resist temptation. God agreed, and that is how Satan first tempted Adam and Eve to approach the forbidden tree. And that is why Satan is always around to tempt us. To avoid this temptation one has to follow the right practice.

from the tree of knowledge; in the *Qur'an*, he accepted knowledge without understanding the consequences; and in both, humans proved to be ignorant and thus arrogant, never realizing the consequences of this action. The will to power is, according to these religions, not innate but incidental to human nature.

The moral duality of human nature is discussed in ancient philosophies as well. Zoroastrianism, for example, views human nature optimistically, although it holds that the force of evil (*Ahriman*) has enormous power to deceive people and tempt them to commit evil deeds. Plato wrote of the same state of "being in between" in his famous allegory of the cave. As the allegory suggests, humanity is not doomed to Hobbes' state of nature, "where every man is enemy to every man" and life is "solitary, poor, nasty, brutish, and short" (Hobbes 1968 [1651], p. 186), but has the potential to go beyond negative temptation and work to enhance good will and encourage proper acts.

Even if we conclude that the will to power is not essential to human nature, we still have to explain the presence of an incidental will to power in humanity. According to Thompson's theory of the security–power dilemma, people find themselves in a lonely and insecure temporal world, whether as a result of God's punishment or a long evolutionary process, and they strive for power to feel secure. Fearing the loss of any power gained, they strive for yet more power. Seen in this way, the will to power is a transitory phase, and it is possible to overcome it. People also strive to cooperate and manage their lives in harmony with others. Applied to politics and polities, this means that the human spirit is capable of both collaboration and discord. It resembles Janus, the two-faced Roman god of mythology.

According to the French political sociologist, Maurice Duverger (1966), politics also has simultaneously the dual faces of order and conflict, collaboration and discord, ministry and competition, management and conflict. Politics has the paradoxical features of harmony and conflict, but this duality manifests itself differently in each epoch or civilizational milieu, owing to the spatiotemporal nature of public life, or what Fernand Braudel (1973) called the *durée*. For example, in the modern secular international system, politics emerged in the guise of security and strategic concerns, particularly during the Cold War, whereas now, in the age of globalization, it has taken the form of primarily economic issues and interactions. In another period, it took on a sacred form of administration by the religious class or of religious wars. However, striving for power is related to some notion of "interest," defined as security or preservation of one's wealth and position. In other words, although the will to power is incidental, concern for interest is always part of human nature. Instead of concentrating on the notion of power, as do the exclusionary approaches outlined above do, one should concentrate on interest and its definition.

The notion of interest defined other than as power generates a different form of politics, which may appear to be more like that of the premodern outlook, yet differs from it. Before the modern state became predominant, the emphasis was on an inclusive notion of interest, defined in terms of the general order of things, rather than in terms of power. With the advent of "political realism," according to Morgenthau, the main signpost for finding our "way through the landscape of international politics is the concept of interest defined in terms of power" (Morgenthau 1978, p. 5). Morgenthau did not say that politics "entails" or "relates to" but definitely "is," because for Morgenthau power is the instigator, the drive, and the immediate goal of politics.

The premodern understanding of interest involved the preservation of a balance between all human beings, between human societies, and even between human societies and nature and the environment — a notion at the base of almost all civilizations up to the time of the Renaissance. Justice was understood as the preservation of a balance in which everything would be in its proper place, rather than as equal rights or equal distribution of goods.[18] From the point of view of ontology, globalization thus invites a new definition of interest. The concept of interest includes the concerns of the individual (human security and rights), groups (women, children, and minorities), states (national interests), regional systems (multilateralism and regionalism), and more importantly the environment (the ecology and biosphere).

From the point of view of epistemology, the end-of-politics paradigm basically operates within the parameters of positivistic science. It accepts only the post-Cartesian doctrine that only sense certainty constitutes theoretical understanding and contributes to fruitful action. It ignores what Charles A. McClelland (1969), a few years ago, called the "wisdom approach." The wisdom approach invites scholars to prudently examine history and appreciate the precarious nature of human conduct, rather than being overwhelmed by masses of data, which more often than not lead to blind spots of partisanship.

Consider, for example, the much-celebrated recent book of Huntington (1996). Based on masses of quotations from various obscure groups and spokespersons in the Islamic world and adopting his end-of-politics approach, Huntington concluded that even in the globalized world, the struggle for power and exclusivity determines the course of politics. Interestingly enough, in his very recent essay, "The Erosion of American National Interest," Huntington (1997b) extended the end-of-politics paradigm to an analysis of national politics in the United States and warned Americans of the danger of the new globalized multicultural trend. The wisdom approach, in contrast, tells us that throughout human history up to the Renaissance and to an important extent in the age of modernity,

---

[18] Justice, for example, was always defined as ordering things according to their nature and, in human society, doing the things one is best suited for. My study of politics and polity in the ancient East, dealing with Mesopotamia, Persia, India, and China, shows that this is the way in which justice was understood regardless of civilizational milieu (Rajaee 1993).

cooperation and collaboration functioned well and power alone was not the predominant variable or the final arbiter in politics.

In his Adam Lord Gifford lectures, Seyyed Hossein Nasr of George Washington University made a strong and convincing case for saying that the natural sciences were always ontologically connected with sacred thinking, until the Renaissance, when the compartmentalization of human understanding began (Nasr 1981). The modern industrialized and competitive world changed our ways of thinking about and organizing the sciences and put forward a framework that began to define politics in terms of power and struggle. The world of industry propagates the notion that "might makes right," and financial success stories create paradigms and accepted norms.

From the phenomenological point of view, the end-of-politics paradigm either ignores the nature of the information revolution or offers a peculiar understanding of it. It sees technology as applied science in the service of those with power and considers it the means for the mighty powers to impose and further enhance their partisan politics and interests. This is contrary to what is really happening, which is a change in the mode and substance of production and therefore in our perceptions of time and space, offering opportunities to create a truly global community.

The case is like that of the industrial revolution, which was not just a gradual use of machines, employment of men and women in factories, and changes in agricultural structure: it was also accompanied by a scientific revolution. So, too, advances in information technology have been accompanied by an information revolution. As Immanuel Kant reminded us in his *Critique of Pure Reason*, one's understanding of time and space shapes one's consciousness. The information revolution and technology have changed our understanding of both time and space. Note the following accurate observation by professor of political philosophy, Tom Darby: "By radically altering the experience of time and space, old worlds become shattered and from the rubble new ones can be fashioned" (Darby 1986, p. iv). The information revolution has changed both the mode and the substance of production, thereby transforming our notions of time and space.

The new mode of production concentrates on services and data processing. What is so important about this mode of production is that it is available to anyone with a basic knowledge of computing and data processing. This meagre requirement has both positive and negative connotations. On the negative side, the manipulation of modern technology to serve particular and parochial ends can have unfortunate consequences. As Kaplan explained, "in places where the Western Enlightenment has not penetrated and where there has always been mass poverty, people find liberation in violence" (1994, p. 72). On the positive side, information technology is much more value free than industry and modernity. As such, it has facilitated the emergence of new classes and groups with a new range of loyalties, rather than an exclusive allegiance to a territorial state.

The new political opportunities, the new economic empowerment, and the weakening of an overarching cultural frame of mind have created new possibilities, which may or may not be used for the greater good. Nevertheless, one has to make the effort. However, I am quite aware that communities, even the new global ones, project contradictory visions. On the one hand, to increase the power of their societies, they promote inclusivist policies. They seem to be aware of the insightful comments of Hannah Arendt:

> Power is never the property of the individual; it belongs to a group and remains in existence only so long as the group keeps together ... . The moment the group from which the power originated to begin with (potestas in populo, without a couple or group there is no power), disappears, "his power" also vanishes.
> — Arendt (1970, p. 44)

The communicative base of power is only possible through the promotion of inclusiveness, by which all members of the society feel a sense of belonging to the community in question. On the other hand, human communities develop exclusivist policies because, as human aggregates, they are afraid of the unknown. Theorists, scholars, and generally "people of the pen" have a moral duty to help remove or diminish this fear, rather than exaggerating it with extremist discourse. The compartmentalized nature of the above approaches, the erroneous conclusion that "might makes right," and the misunderstanding that information technology is merely a means all encourage exclusivist policies, in one form or another. A more complex approach could foster an inclusive discourse and a participatory context to enable collaboration rather than discord to flourish in the future.

43

CIVILIZATIONAL APPROACH,
THE RESTORATION OF POLITICS

Here, I propose a complex, integrative approach, which rests on the assumption that truth is a multilayered phenomenon, contrary to the other approaches to the investigation of the human condition, which either suggest that truth does not exist at all or that there is only one method to obtain it. The complex approach takes the story of the elephant and the dark room as its guide in the quest for truth. This story was narrated by the Muslim mystic, Jalal ad-Din Rumi (1207–73):

> *The elephant was in a dark house: some Hindus had brought it for exhibition. In order to see it, many people were going, every one, into that darkness. As seeing it with the eye was impossible, [each one] was feeling it in the dark with the palm of his hand. The hand of another touched its ear: to him it appeared to be like a fan. Since another handled its leg, he said, "I found the elephant's shape to be like a pillar." Another laid his hand on its back: he said, "Truly, this elephant was like a throne." Similarly, whenever anyone heard (a description of the elephant), he understood (it only in respect of) the part that he had touched. If there had been a candle in each one's hand, the difference would have gone out of their words.*
>
> — Jalal ad-Din Rumi (1977,
> book III, lines 1259–1268)

The complex approach maintains that each one of the exclusionary approaches, or paradigms, used in the study of the human condition presents a mere facet of the complex reality of human nature and society. At the same time, each may provide us with some insight into the human condition in the global age.

Thus, one should both appreciate and criticize these approaches. One learns from them because each concentrates on an important aspect of being human, but one should avoid them for the same reason: any one-dimensional approach is bound to lead to exclusivism. As the history professor, John Gaddis (1999, p. 74), recently observed, "the essence of politics is the balancing of priorities, and this requires an ecological perspective — a sense of the whole, along with the sensitivity to how things relate to one another. That seems to be missing as we approach the twenty-first century." Globalization is simultaneously political, economic, and sociocultural. Each approach takes us closer to an understanding of one of these aspects. The following defines it best: globalization is "a complex set of distinct but related processes — economic, cultural, social and also political and military — through which social relations have developed towards a global scale and with global reach, over a long historic period" (Shaw 1997, p. 498). Similar to other historical phenomena, these processes move in a paradoxical fashion. They integrate and fragment, create opportunities and present dangers, homogenize and lead to heterogeneity, and universalize and localize. This paradox of fragmentation and integration is rightly termed "fragmegration" (Rosenau 1998, p. 37). Globalization is a double movement, affecting all aspects of human life, as well as all regions of the world, for both better and worse. Technology has caused the formation of a historical system, and the double movement has presented the new outlook of globalism. The alliance of the two has led to the emergence of a new phase in human civilization, that is, one global civilization containing many civilizations.

The complex, integrative approach seeks to revive and restore politics to its original status as the "master science" in understanding the human condition here on Earth. Technology enables humanity to take a holistic view of the planet. To understand the human condition requires a similar holistic approach, as elaborated in "the Aristotelian project" (Neufeld 1995), which bases the understanding of the human condition on two variables: the person, as the actor, and the *polis*, as the setting in which the person's potentials are actualized. I operate with the assumption that globalization has made one *polis* out of the Earth and that this should help to determine our understanding of its politics and governance. Moreover, my argument begins with the Platonic insight that "the city is the soul writ large" (Plato 1948, 368–369) and that the new city created by globalization is the soul writ large on the global scale, containing the whole world and affecting every member of the human race.

To understand this comprehensive phenomenon, I operate with a unique set of ontological assumptions, as opposed to compartmentalized views and approaches. Here, my argument begins with the Aristotelian assumption that "man is by nature an animal intended to live in a *polis*. He who is without a *polis*, by reason of his own nature and not of some accident, is either a poor sort of being, or a being higher than man" (Aristotle 1958, 1253a; see also Aristotle 1979, 169b). Being human only makes sense within the context of an aggregate or a polity, whether the unit is a tribe, clan, city-state (the *polis*), country, nation-state, empire, civilization, or, now, the globe. The concept of the *polis* is very important. In ancient Greece, it was a community simultaneously comprising state, society, economy, religion, and culture — or a way of life. As will be shown, the notion of the *polis* resembles what I refer to here as a civilization. Globalization has created an *oikomene* and an organization of the people of the Earth, who act and speak together. Similar to the *polis* — which did not equalize people but created equal opportunity — it has given everyone some form and degree of opportunity. Arendt described the function of the *polis* as follows: "Isonomy guaranteed ... equality, but not because all men were born or created equal, but, on the contrary, because men were by nature ... not equal" (Arendt 1963, p. 23). The *polis* creates a sense of equality. Similarly, globalization creates a sense of political space and a global public sphere, enabling many people to feel empowered.

It may be argued that this ontology presupposes a cosmological worldview in which the sacred and the profane still share the same path and therefore that it may be inapplicable to a world where these realms have long been divided. Even a non-monotheist may argue that, because I, the author, am a monotheist, my belief system surely colours my ontological assumption. Two points are in order here. First, no doubt I began with a religious and normative conviction, but the course of the inquiry proved to me that the comprehensive, integrative approach allows for monotheistic, polytheistic, and even nontheistic norms. In other words, it invites a complex understanding of the ways rationality pervades human theoretical and practical discourse and implies that the production of civilization results from their balanced interaction. Second, as already shown, our less comprehensive understanding of the human condition results from considering the sacred and the secular as separate and contradictory, rather than contrary.

An exposé of two variables — the human (that is, the microcosm) and the civilizational milieu (that is, the macrocosm) — will show the universal applicability of the civilizational framework. Human beings are the main actors, and, for now, the global community is the main arena for the expression of human potential. Just as the individual strives to materialize his or her potential, the *polis* and, now, civilization enable collective potentials to be thoroughly actualized. It is in this context that Aristotle (1958, 1253a) claimed that "justice belongs to the *polis*." The interaction of the two, the microcosm and macrocosm, lies at the heart of human existence, intellectual endeavours, and civilizational achievements.

To understand the new phase of human existence, one has to begin with the same two variables: the human and the civilizational milieu (the human's public sphere). A discussion of human nature begins, first and foremost, with the assumption that we are both divine and secular and that our condition is best described using Plato's term *metaxy*, or "in between." Our secular aspect contains the political, economic, scientific, and cultural realms, whereas our sacred aspect contains the ethical, moral, and transcendental realms. Thus, we have a sophisticated nature that is also attracted to perfection (*Homo religiosus*), curious to discover and make new things (*Homo faber*), and overtaken with interest and thus the desire for power (*Homo dominandis*). The combination of these three tendencies, regulated by three corresponding forms of rationality — normative, positive, and utilitarian — makes a human being whatever he or she may be. The balanced functioning of these aspects of human nature empowers us to create and produce civilization.

Table 2 captures the argument so far and presents an anatomy of human ontology and the combined, yet distinct and contrary (but not contradictory) components of human nature functioning integratively to produce an active and dynamic person. This table presents an alternative to the unidimensional understanding of human nature and the way its contrary dimensions interact. This is a gender- and race-free analogy and concentrates on one and only one aspect of the human soul, namely, its being human.

This three-dimensional view captures the dynamic nature of a human being. Time and place and the individual's civilizational milieu determine which aspect plays a more dominant role. Table 3 captures how the components of human nature manifest themselves in a polity, or social context, whether a tribe, city, country, or, as a result of globalization, the world. Indeed, globalization has now made the world that context. It has brought all previous civilizations and other world visions into its historical system and has made them actors and contributors to the one commonwealth of humanity.

Table 2. The microcosm — the soul.

Categories	Spheres		
	Spiritus (spirit)	*Mens* (mind)	Passion (sense)
Domain of being (*mundos*)	*Metaphysica imaginalis* (images)	Physics (nature) *Speculatium* (speculation)	*Polis dominandis* (ruling)
Rationality	Normative	Positive	Utilitarian
Mode of operation	Contemplation	Investigation	Trial and error
Means	Intellect	Reason	*Ration*
End (*telos*)	Wonder	Comprehension	Balance
Product	*Nomos* (ethics and customs)	*Mythos* (explanation of nature)	*Cosmos* (order in the polity)

Source: This is the author's mapping of the parts of the soul and their ontological manifestation.

The civilizational approach provides the broadest context for these various human aspects to manifest themselves and makes it possible for them to interact as a totality. Indeed, civilizations operate on the basis of a triangle of spirit, mind, and senses, producing normative, positive, and utilitarian forms of rationality, with a corresponding triangle of *nomos, mythos,* and *cosmos.* Note that the analogy of the triangle also suggests that the spiritual, mental, and sensory aspects are connected through these three forms of rationality, which make a human what she or he is, a rational being. Only as a result of the simultaneous functioning of these forms of rationality does life have a solid foundation, make sense, and prove worthy of living and sometimes worth dying for.

To make sense of this ontology, one needs to more fully understand the notion of civilization as a polity. To clarify this notion, I address the following questions: What is civilization? What does a civilization do? When is a civilization born? How long does a civilization flourish? How does globalization compare with the Islamic and modern Western civilizations? Let the masters be our guide in such an inquiry.

Table 3. The macrocosm — the polity (civilization).

Categories	Spheres		
	Sacred	Knowledge	Action
Actors	Priest and artist	Philosopher and scientist	Politician and merchant
Discourse	Religion and art	Philosophy and science	Politics and economics
Modus operandi	Propagation and creation	Speculation and conjecture	Persuasion and production
End (*telos*)	Norms (vice and virtue)	Proposition (truth and falsity)	Utility (interest and loss)
Product	Serenity	Certainty	Satisfaction

Note: This is the author's epistemological mapping of the functioning of the three parts of the soul in the polity, which result from the three disciplines of religion, science, and politics.

WHAT IS CIVILIZATION?

In an important essay entitled "The History of Civilizations: The Past Explains the Present," Braudel (1980) invited his readers to a meeting of great minds, like Jacob Burckhardt, François Guizot, Oswald Spengler, Arnold Toynbee, and Philip Bagby. For Braudel, the terms *civilization* and *culture* are closely linked and sometimes interchangeable. He wrote, "A civilization, we say, is a collection of cultural characteristics and phenomena" (Braudel 1980, p. 77), and he continued,

> A civilization is first of all a space, a "cultural area," as the anthropologists would say, a locus. Within that locus which may be more or less extensive but is never too confined, you must picture a great variety of "goods," of cultural characteristics, ranging from the form of its houses, the material of which they are built, their roofing, to skills like feathering arrows, to a dialect or a group of dialects, to tastes in cooking, to a particular technology, a structure of beliefs, a way of making love, and even to the compass, paper, the printing press ... . If to this spatial coherence can be added some sort of temporal permanence, then I would call civilization or culture the "totality" of the range of attributes.
>
> — Braudel (1980, p. 202)

Although civilization and culture are closely linked, they should not be taken as synonymous. As will become clear, civilization is asymmetrically related to culture. Civilization is the more general category, whereas culture is the more particular one. Although civilizations each have a sophisticated culture, not all cultures have become or produced a civilization.

I will say more on this later, but for now Toynbee's definition is important because for Toynbee a civilization is an "intelligible field of historical study" (Toynbee 1934, vol. I, p. 51). Only through the investigation of civilization is the venture of humanity revealed *in toto*, whereas other units of study reveal only some of its parts. As Toynbee put it, "I mean by civilization, the smallest unit of historical study to which one is brought when trying to *comprehend* the history of one's country" (Toynbee 1934, cited in Braudel 1980, p. 190, emphasis in the original). Note that a civilization is considered a mirror of the age-old achievements of a country.

Ibn Khaldun's definition, which Braudel ignored in his review, conveys a similar understanding. Ibn Khaldun defined the concept of civilization in the following passage:

> *Human social organization is something necessary. The philosophers expressed this fact by saying "Man is political by nature." That is, he cannot do without the social organization for which the philosophers use the technical term "town" (polis). This is what civilization means.*
>
> — Ibn Khaldun (1958, vol. I, p. 89)

Ibn Khaldun equated civilization with the "*polis*" in the Greek sense. As mentioned, I think it is an accurate picture because the *polis* is more than a political power base, an economic unit, or a social context (Voegelin 1956). It is a self-contained community and performs the three functions of political order, economic welfare, and a cultural framework and provides for its members an ethical paradigm, a sense of meaning, and a *modus operandi*. As Cox (1995, p. 11) explained, "civilizations are ways of being, ways of understanding the world, ways of acting upon that understanding. They shape people's perceptions and thus how they react to events." Whereas Cox added that they "exist in the realm of intersubjectivity," and the level of abstraction is extremely important, I think the objective realm, or the realm of "material values," to use Braudel's (1980) expression, is important, too. As will be shown, civilizations contain both material and nonmaterial conditions of being. Indeed, I would like to accept Cox's double notion of process and condition, according to which civilization "refers to a process of becoming civilized and to a condition of being civilized" (Cox 1995, p. 11). To guarantee the first, one has to produce material "values," and to remain civilized, one has to increase intersubjective relations.

51

WHAT DOES A CIVILIZATION DO?

Civilization is the highest stage of a human attempt to produce social "life" or a dynamic condition allowing for the concomitant production of what humanity considers valuable, or "values." I use *value* in its plural form, having in mind David Easton's (1953, p. 129) famous definition of politics as "authoritative allocation of values." According to Easton, politics is the art of distributing all values — economic, political, social, and cultural — in an authoritative fashion so that no member of the community feels left out. These values are produced by the various organizational forms that humanity has invented, but they reach their ultimate productivity in a coordinated manner within the parameters of a civilization. Thus, the concept of civilization refers to a condition that enables the concomitant production of power, wealth, social and cultural interaction, and innovation. It also includes scientific discovery and invention, artistic and aesthetic creativity, and even mythical and magical generation and regeneration, as parts of the productive process. In this capacity, civilizations establish a paradigm, provide meaning, and provide the *modus operandi* for their members. As a member of a civilization, one has a sense of identity, belonging, and purposeful life. Civilizations set the boundaries for rights, privileges, and responsibilities.

WHEN IS A CIVILIZATION BORN?

Political scientist Mehdi Mozaffari suggested that civilizations materialize when a world vision and a historical system come together. The historical system, for Mozaffari, is an empirical reality, whereas a world vision is an abstract idea:

> When a historical system is realized without being based on a comprehensive world vision, the formation gives rise to tribes, empires, states and other forms of political entities, but not civilizations. Similarly, when a world vision stands without a body, a "physical" shape, it is merely an ideology, a culture or a religion.
>
> — Mozaffari (1998a, pp. 4–5)

Whereas Mozaffari provided no examples, a few would be helpful. The most obvious example of a historical system that failed to become a civilization would be that of the Mongols. The Mongolian leader Genghis Khan (*d.* 1227) began the impressive march of his horsemen toward the West, and his kinsmen advanced it through the Persian plateau and all the way to Jerusalem. Based on the Mongolian legal system of *yassa*, which defined the rights and obligations of the elite and provided theoretical justification for their new order, a world system was created. This system lasted for about a century but was never translated into a civilization. The opposite example would be that of Taoism, which presented a sophisticated and important Chinese world vision but has remained a religion and a culture.

Long before Mozaffari, Max Weber (1958b) argued that modern capitalism was born of a junction between the Protestant world vision and the emerging European bourgeois capitalist system. Weber and Mozaffari both concluded that the interaction of a general theory and a practical system would lead to the formation of a civilization. It is difficult to accept this as a general rule, however, as there are historical cases where such a junction occurred but did not evolve into a civilization. In the 4th century, Constantine made Christianity the official religion of the Roman Empire, thus joining a world vision with a sophisticated historical system, but that neither saved Rome from falling nor created a new civilization. Similarly, in the 6th century,

the Persian Sassanid King Qobad made Mazdakism and its
world vision the official religion of the empire, but this neither
enhanced the Mazdakis' vision nor helped the crumbling
empire. In more recent times, the Marxist world vision and the
Soviet historical system were joined, but the result was a political system that survived by means of repression, lasted less than
a century, and never produced a civilization.

I feel the joining of theory and practice is important, and
no doubt, to paraphrase Benedictus de Spinoza (1632–77),
things never happen in fact unless they happen in the world of
ideas. But history tells us that the mere joining of a historical
system with a world vision does not lead to a civilization. In
recent history, Pan-Islamism, Pan-Arabism, Pan-Westism, and
Ba'thism have been adopted by, or imposed on, the Middle
Eastern historical systems, and each of these experiments failed
to produce a workable civilization. The formation of a civilization needs much more than a historical system and a world
vision. Only when and if the joining of a world vision and a historical system leads to the concomitant production of a set of
values is a civilization born of this union. The impetus for its
creation is found in a paradoxical mixture of solidarity and liberty. A strong feeling of attachment and the readiness to offer
sacrifices for the cause of both the vision and the historic system
guarantee and solidify a civilization; liberty to innovate and to
create ensures its survival and endurance.

Ibn Khaldun observed that the foundation of a new state is
solidarity. By that, he meant a strong feeling of bonding with,
and loyalty toward, a group and its goals, to the point that the
members would fight and even sacrifice their lives for the
advancement of its cause. At the same time, individual members
should feel free to think and critically ponder over the society
they live in.[19] In short, for civilizations to function they require
relatively uncontested rules of the game (the law), authoritative

53

---

[19]   In a Persian essay, I developed the complex relationship of individual,
liberty, society, and solidarity as a system for producing life. See Farhang
Rajaee (1998).

institutions (allocating values), and, more importantly, civic, communal, and corporate dispositions. These dispositions include a preparedness to appreciate others who may define the rules of the game differently. This takes the discussion to the question of the longevity of civilizations.

HOW LONG DOES A CIVILIZATION FLOURISH?

Civilizations continue to flourish as long as they can respond to challenges, which come either from the past or from the future. Indeed, creativity and productivity take place at the juncture of past and future, which requires an art of balancing between, to quote Max Weber, "the eternal yesterday" (1958a, p. 78) and, *à la* Weber, "the eternal tomorrow." The former generates legitimacy, and the latter generates efficiency. A proper response to the pressures of the eternal yesterday guarantees moral and political authority, and a proper response to the demands of the eternal tomorrow adds to the efficacy and power of a given civilization. This makes a civilization flourish. Without this condition and framework, the members of a civilization feel unproductive, useless, and alienated and have the sense that their identities are shattered. In this respect, all civilizations are the result of renewal and regeneration.

One of the lasting impressions of my graduate studies was made by the leading authority on international organizations and theories, Inis Claude, Jr, when he remarked that Adam was the only soul who could claim originality. It was not because of Adam's genius but because there was no one else before him. No civilization can claim to have brought forth something absolutely novel. In fact, the enduring civilizations have been those that combined a contemporary view of the eternal yesterday and proper innovation to respond to the demands of the eternal tomorrow.

Two examples may help to clarify the point. The first is the Islamic civilization, which at present, is in a state of decay, and the second is Western civilization, which, according to many, is degenerating.

The Islamic civilization was born in the 9th century, when its world vision joined a historical system and was thereby able to concomitantly produce power, wealth, and culture. Its world vision was the revealed message of Islam, and its historical system was an ingenious synthesis of Arab, Roman, and Persian legacies. The combination produced a world that had its own internal cohesion, local specificity, and universal appeal. It was truly a global–local phenomenon. A political historian of the Middle East, Albert Hourani, captured the character of this world in the following passage:

55

> The life of the famous traveller Ibn Battuta (1304c.–1377) illustrates the links between the cities and lands of Islam. His pilgrimage, undertaken when he was twenty-one years old, was only the beginning of a life of wandering. It took him from his native city of Tangiers in Morocco to Mecca by way of Syria; then to Baghdad and southwestern Iran; to Yemen, east Africa, Oman and the [Persian] Gulf; to Asia Minor, the Caucasus, and southern Russia; to India, the Maldive Islands and China; then back to his native Maghrib, and from there to Andalus and the Sahara. Wherever he went, he visited the tombs of saints and frequented scholars, with whom he was joined by the link of a common culture expressed in the Arabic language. He was well received at the courts of princes, and by some of them appointed to the office of qadi [judge]; this honor, conferred on him as far from home as Delhi and Maldive Islands, showed the prestige attached to the exponents of the religious learning in the Arabic tongue.
> — Hourani (1991, p. 129)

After the Mongol invasion of the Islamic world in the 13th century and despite its enormous destruction of the urban centres and civilizational bastions, Islam as a civilizational unit regenerated itself at the beginning of the 16th century. This time, the Islamic world vision joined the Central Asian, Indian, Persian, and Turkish historical system, and this resulted in what Marshal Hodgson (1974) called the three "gunpowder empires" — those of the Mughals of India (1526–1857), the Safavids of Persia (1501–1736), and the Ottomans of Anatolia

(1301–1923).[20] These empires represented the last of the Islamic world as a living and dynamic civilization. Each regenerated itself on the basis of its understanding of the Islamic world vision, and each was able to produce a world system that concomitantly produced values and left legacies that still define identities in these regions. A serious problem occurred, however: their responses to the demands of the eternal tomorrow relied too heavily on the past. They continued to base their societies on the agrarian mode of production, a strategy becoming obsolete with the coming of modernity and the industrial mode of production. Not surprisingly, therefore, each lost its internal balance in its encounter with the industrial civilizations of the West. The whole Islamic world has faced a crisis of productivity ever since. When Napoleon invaded Egypt in 1798, it was more than a political failure of the Islamic stronghold. It also symbolized its inability to produce power, wealth, and culture.

The Muslims completely abandoned hope of regenerating or renewing their civilization, and in the first decades of the century it seemed that the solution was to imitate the West in every way, as was the policy of Mustafa Kemal Ataturk in Turkey and Reza Shah in Iran. Seyyed Hassan Taqizadeh (1878–1970), a sophisticated Iranian intellectual, revolutionary activist, statesman, historian, philologist, essayist, and modernist, aptly described the idea in the following words: the solution to the crisis of Iran was "unconditional acceptance and emanation of European civilization, and absolute submission to Europe and the adaptation of its mores and customs ... . [In short,] Iran has to become Europeanized in appearance, essence, physical features and spiritual aspects. There is no other way" (Taqizadeh 1920, p. 1). The dramatic resurgence of Islam in recent decades

[20] Turkish nomads settled in Asia Minor in about 1243. In 1281, Osman Bey (1259–1326) became the leader, and in 1301 he declared himself sultan and established the Ottoman Empire. The conquest of Selim I (ruled 1465–1520) brought to the Ottomans the tradition of the Abbasid Caliphate, and their status suddenly grew to that of a world power. Under Suleyman the Magnificent (ruled 1520–66), the expansion was even faster, and the Ottoman Empire more or less became a world power. The Ottomans ruled for seven centuries, until Mustafa Kemal Ataturk and the new republic abolished the sultanate and the caliphate in 1923.

led to the first classic social, political, and economic revolution outside the Western cultural *oikoumene*, namely the Islamic revolution in Iran in 1979. This was indeed a reaction to that earlier solution and an attempt to revive the Islamic heritage.

The other example of the need to combine a view of the eternal yesterday with an innovative response to the eternal tomorrow is the modern West. The base of this civilization is the renaissance, or "rebirth," of the eternal yesterday of the Greek, Roman, and Islamic heritage. The prominent historian, William McNeill (1963), went as far as to suggest that the eternal yesterday of the West is human experience as a whole, from the beginning of citied life in Mesopotamia to the time of the megacities of North America and Europe. Its renewal has created a "world anew." The economic heritage of the industrial revolution dictated the industrial mode of production; the political heritage of the French revolution brought about pluralistic democracy; the Italian Renaissance led the project of modernity; and their combination provided the political, economic, and sociocultural dimensions of a new civilization. Gradually, the whole world embraced it, and what we now know as the international system was born. One can make an observation similar to that of the ancient Muslim traveler, Ibn Battuta (as portrayed in Hourani 1991), but about a traveler going through various parts of the West or even the world, today: It is a world in which the English language predominates. One can travel throughout this world, feel welcomed, and have one's talents recognized and appreciated.

As in the Islamic civilizational milieu, however, the West has begun to show signs of excess, but in reverse. Although the West continues to concurrently produce political, economic, and social values, its links with its eternal yesterday are weakening. It is even advocating a break with the past, failing to heed Heinrich Freyer's warning that "the kingdom of reason has its beginnings in the kingdom of God" (from Freyer's famous *Weltgeshichte Europas*, vol. 2, p. 723, cited in Braudel 1980, p. 199). The West appears to have far too much faith in the eternal tomorrow.

How does globalization compare with the Islamic and modern Western civilizations?

Globalization has inaugurated a new process and condition. In some ways it has renewed the past, and in others it has been innovative and initiative. One interesting way to compare them would be to look at the ways each one views the "others." Generally speaking, the "others" refers to those who do not conform to a given civilization's world vision or ideals. For example, the Aryans of India called the others "untouchables"; the Iranians, the "Aniranis"; the Greeks, the "barbarians"; and the monotheistic civilizations, the "infidels." The modern industrial civilization labels the others "primitive," "uncivilized," "traditional," "undeveloped," and "backward." What is interesting is that usually the term also refers to the civilization that preceded the one currently in a position of power and production. For instance, for the Aryans, the others were the hunters and gatherers who hunted and killed the animals vital to the Aryans' agrarian economy. A curse from the sacred books of Avesta, the Zoroastrian scriptures, underlines the point: "Mazda [the appellation of God in Zoroastrianism] will curse those who slaughter animals with happiness" (cited in Rajaee 1993, p. 75). The hunting and gathering mode of production proved to be the biggest enemy of the new agrarian paradigm. Later, industrial society, using the same formula, condemned those who hung on to the age-old traditions of the previous civilization and failed to heed the creed of modernity — that the individual is the true measure of all things.

Nowhere do the differences among civilizations manifest themselves more than in the types of humour they produce. When I first arrived in Oklahoma in the 1970s, what struck me most was that humour revolved around the "aggies," the farmers bound to the traditional ways of life. For example, it would always take five aggies to change a light bulb and so on. What is interesting about globalization is that the "others" refers to those who have not submitted to its ways. Because this mode of "civilization production" has captured the entire globe, the "others" are the aliens from an unknown planet. The "others" are the extraterrestrials. The humour of this phase of human civilization is also of the same type. Consider the character of Mr Bean, portrayed by the British actor Rowan Atkinson. Every episode of his show begins with a beam of light from which he is dropped from an unknown destination. But the humour itself is important and telling of our global civilization. It is a kind of humour that offends no one. It is not targeting any ethnic, religious, cultural, or civilizational group — the humour is humane.

Globalization is the regeneration and renewal of the industrial civilization in a new and expanded form. Technology has become a more expanded and sophisticated version of industry but is also based on it, and information has become an expanded and more sophisticated version of scientific mode of rationality but is also based on it. The mode of production in this new regeneration is that of information. It has created its own elite and has broadened the context of our very existence. What does this entail?

First, it has increased the number of actors in the public arena. It used to be assumed that only the state was privileged to play a role in international politics. That privilege is now given to international institutions (whether governmental or non-governmental), private corporations (which operate at the global level and are widely known as either multinational or transnational corporations), individuals, and above all the media. The last are paramount because they control the means of "information production" at their disposal, set the agenda, define the terms of the discourse, and change the debate. It is interesting to compare the media people in our time with the feudal lords and landed aristocracy of the agrarian age and the capitalists, executives, and bourgeoisie of the industrial age.

Second, the new mode of production has introduced new rules of the game. When the high-tech company, Microsoft, decided to build a new laboratory, it looked all over the globe for a location and decided on Cambridge, in the United

59

Kingdom, for its headquarters. In other words, a firm's national loyalty is only important as long as it does not alienate its international constituency of investors. The states and international law can produce, manage, and control global governance only up to a point. Moreover, international law is a body of rules set by the states for the states, and the states modify these rules whenever they deem it necessary. A new way of setting the rules of the game has to be worked out to serve the new global players. For example, the World Trade Organization (WTO) is responsible for setting the rules of the game for international trade, finance, and exchange.

Third, the information revolution has produced a new arena, or public sphere, one that is truly global: the World Wide Web, or Internet. The paradoxical feature of the new rules of the game is that they make the main distinctions between national and international, inside and outside, universal and particular, and local and global no longer as clear as they once were. Any rearticulation of political time and space must assume a close linkage of the national and international contexts, move the rules of the game away from the notion of "either—or" toward that of "both—and," and make these rules bear the mark of the "local—global." Why should the new rules have this paradoxical feature? Part of the answer lies in the complex picture presented by the holistic, integrative approach to understanding human nature and its relations to its civilizational milieu. Part of the answer can be found in the main characteristics of the new global context, to be addressed in the following chapter.

One word of caution before I continue. The main features of the civilizational approach should not be taken as what anthropologists call "ascriptive characteristics," that is, attributes and categories that remain stable and require no revision. Even if human aspirations and desires remain constant, their interaction with the new creation, based on the demand to comprehend the eternal tomorrow, makes their temporal actualization require constant revision, new understanding, reconstruction, and sometimes restoration. The civilizational approach is a learning device and a comprehensive conjecture, and these features enable it to respond to many of the short-comings of the more extreme approaches to the study of the human condition.

The Coming of the Information Civilization

Modernity transforms all existing civilizations, including that of the West. It is not Westernization, but a universal change in the fundamental conditions of any and all civilizations.
— David Gress (1997, p. 526)

The union of communication technology and computer data processing has affected most of the ways humanity has been conducting its affairs recently. Has this changed our social framework? Wisdom has it that this depends on whether these developments have affected the mode of production, as that would in turn influence both our ways of doing things and our ways of thinking. What does the phrase, "mode of production," mean, or, as a phenomenon, what does it signify? To answer this question, I turn to history. When Karl Marx (1818–83) and Friedrich Engels (1820–95) explored the origins of the state, they focused their attention on the ownership of the means of production as their main variable. But they ran into an anomaly, namely, Asian societies, which had communal ownership of land. In these societies, they found a sophisticated social stratification and a state power structure that generated, distributed, and exercised power; controlled and used economic resources; and fostered a sense of solidarity, real or imagined, among its subjects. Marx and Engels could explain this phenomenon through neither slave ownership nor the feudal modes of production.

They hypothesized that there could be a variety of modes of production, such as "the ancient," "the Slavic," and "the Germanic," and formulated the notion of the "Asiatic mode of production" to explain the origin and development of Asian societies (Godelier 1978). Based on elaboration of these various modes of production, Marx and Engels concluded that the "mode of production" refers to a sophisticated web of interaction in a given society used to meet its material needs, as well as its more important need for meaning. A society's mode of production provides meaning through, for example, the ownership of the means of production, the mechanisms and the rules of the game, and the idea of "exchange value," which together facilitate the administration of civil affairs in a polity, are held in common, and are open to public scrutiny and judgment. The mode of production shapes the form that society takes. For instance, an agrarian mode results in a feudal state, whereas an industrial mode creates a bourgeois one.

What could one say of the mode of production under globalization? What are the institutional mechanisms for arbitrating, implementing, and regulating the affairs of the new global civilization? On the one hand, various non-Western traditional players demand "a new economic order," "a new cultural order," and even "a new communication order." On the other hand, newly emerging actors such as nongovernmental organizations (NGOs), as well as various advocates of environmental protection and minority rights, promote other agendas. Their combined force has modified some of the existing rules and is in the process of modifying others.

What is valuable in the global marketplace today? It seems that information has replaced previous values in the market. For example, the changing mode of economic production has caused a steep decline in the price of such important raw materials as petroleum. For example, the price of oil was about $3.00 a barrel before it jumped to more than $11.00 in 1973. It then rose to about $40.00 before the Islamic revolution in Iran in 1979 (Rauscher 1989). Then there was a decrease in oil price during the 1980s, to a single digit, but it increased again in the late 1990s. The average price set by the Organization of Petroleum Exporting Countries for oil in 1998 was $12.28 a barrel (Rauscher 1998). Information has become the standard in the realm of exchange value, replacing gold and raw materials. Humanity has evolved from the industrial to the information age.

Our historical evolution to this new phase has not, however, made the previous frameworks or *modus operandi* outmoded. It has made new ones to constitute the prevalent paradigm, which combines the past with the present and has been accepted because it is much more effective, more relevant to our life today, and easy to apply and use. What are the features of this new society? How does the new mode of production differ from the industrial one? What does the information revolution signify? What are the features of the new civilization? How do these changes affect our functioning in the political, economic, and public realms? These are questions that guide the discussion in this chapter. They address, however, the main frame of reference of our time, namely, the information civilization. It was earlier suggested that the combination of technology and the information revolution has been the main impetus for the unfolding of the new phase of human civilization. Thus, this chapter concentrates on the nature of technological society and the meaning of the information revolution and proceeds with the issues pertaining to the functioning of the new information civilization.

TECHNOLOGICAL SOCIETY

Today, technology is our way of being. The German thinker Ernst Junger (1895–1998) went so far as to call it the real metaphysics of the 20th century (Wilkinson 1964). Other scholars equate technology with applied science, as a mere means to an end. However, technology is neither a new invention nor the result of modern science. In the *Nicomachean Ethics*, Aristotle referred to skills, arts, crafts, and general know-how as the means by which people create certain products (Aristotle 1979). People have used both processes and products to cope with, and change, their environment. In general, technology seems to be the *how* that links the *what is* (science, social science) to *what should be* (humanities, religion) (Lisensky et al. 1985).

In this sense, different types of technologies emerge with different forms of civilization. The hunter—gatherer, the agrarian, and the industrial civilizations each produced their own technologies. What has changed in modern times is that "know-how" has become a way of life. When know-how joined the industrial mode of production (*Homo faber*), the mechanical modes of thinking and discourse became dominant. *To make* became the most revered verb in the dominant parlance. *To make money, to make things work, to make events happen, to make jobs, to make a living*, etc. replaced all those terms that expressed the inclusion of humanity as a part in a greater being, rather than being the master, able to create or destroy. Indeed, Hobbes went as far as to claim that all existence, including human existence, is mechanical, as explicitly stated in the introduction to the *Leviathan*: "For what is *Heart*, but a *Spring*; and the *Nerves*, but so many *Strings*; and the *Joynts*, but so many *Wheels*, giving motion to the whole Body" (Hobbes 1968 [1651], p. 81, emphasis in the original). Thus, humanity was to imitate this mechanical structure of nature and make mechanical tools to dominate nature and mechanical social engineering to control fellow human beings. It was up to humanity to *invent* a social framework to make its social organization work properly. No longer would higher forces such as God or the natural order be helpful.

Although it took two centuries for the idea to become the accepted paradigm, when it did (in the 19th century), it became the dominant faith. In Neil Postman's view, "Alfred North Whitehead summed it up best when he remarked that the greatest invention of the nineteenth century was the idea of invention itself" (Postman 1992, p. 42). Invention, progress, evolution, advancement, command, and control dominated discourse, not just in areas devoted to the satisfaction of human essential needs, but also in the realm of the production of meaning and civilization. The industrial revolution gradually led to industrial society and later industrial civilization, as the notion of "how" dominated all aspects of life. For example, the central question of politics changed from "who should rule" to "how to rule"; and in the realm of production, from "what to produce" to "how to best exploit the resources." The obvious response to this situation was for people to try to find the best way to dominate nature (exploitation of resources), manipulate the forces of nature (water, wind, and solar energies), and control and manipulate historical evolution (historicism and philosophy of history). The invention or redefinition of the various educational disciplines was to promote such objectives: natural science for manipulating natural resources, social sciences for social engineering and scientific management, philosophy of history not only for discovering "the rule" of human venture but for guiding the reshaping of the future — even philosophy was not to explain things but to change them. Technocracy, bureaucracy, and democracy relied on science to help in the scientific management of production, administration, and governance.

67

Today, many social critics feel that it has gone too far and that technology has come to dominate humanity. Postman (1992, p. 48) called this state of affairs "technopoly," which he defined as "totalitarian technocracy." But that is a bit of an exaggeration. Technology is neither a mere instrument nor a comprehensive cultural system. It is both, and as a result, it is in great demand everywhere in the world. A look at our daily lives demonstrates the point. People have their radios, stereos, televisions, air conditioners, fans, and similar appliances on from the minute they come in the house, not because they need them or want to use them, but because these constitute their very

existence. Ellul (1964, p. xxv) defined technology as "the totality of methods rationally arrived at and having absolute efficiency in every field of human activity." Or as Hunter (1992,
p. 26) put it, "technology is not just used, it is lived."

This is why many scholars use the phrase "technical society," and some devote their life to the study of it. The most
prominent such scholar is the French philosopher Jacques Ellul
(1912–94), who heralded the coming of "the technological society" before the information revolution.[21] Unlike industry, technology has certain unique features that make it easy to be
adopted in various cultural settings. Technological society works
on the basis of technique, which for Ellul equates with science.
He wrote, "I often use the term *technique* in the place of the
commonly used term *science*" (1964, p. 11). He even saw technique as broader than science: "science has become an instrument of technique" (1964, p. 10). What is the effect of
technique? Based on Ellul's work, Fasching summarized it as
follows:

> *The characteristics of technique which serve to make efficiency a*
> *necessity are rationality, artificiality, automatism of technical choice,*
> *self-augmentation, monism, universalism, and autonomy. The*
> *rationality of technique enforces logical and mechanical organization*
> *through division of labor, the setting of production standard, etc. And*
> *it creates an artificial system which "eliminates or subordinates the*
> *natural world."*
>
> — Fasching (1981, p. 17)

As the industrial revolution became a universal phenomenon, for example, the idea of applying scientific rules to society
gained currency. At that time, Frederick Winslow Taylor
(1856–1915) developed his theory of scientific management; he
was, at the time, working at Midvale Steel in New York. Out of
his Midvale Steel experiments studying the amount of time that

---

[21] Jacques Ellul was born in Bordeaux, France, on 6 January 1912. During the mid-1930s, he was a member of the French Communist Party, and he
then fought with the French Resistance during World War II. He taught at
Bordeaux law school and at its Institute of Political Studies. He wrote
43 books, mostly about theology and ethics. He was concerned about main-
taining moral values in a technological society. He died in May of 1994, in
Bordeaux.

each worker was spending to perform a particular function, Taylor came up with a set of guidelines to enable management to increase the productivity of labour by making it more efficient (Taylor 1947). His formula became the accepted norm for assembly lines, although behavioural approaches later modified it.

Mass production in a dual sense of "increase in productivity" and "for mass consumption" has led to another feature of the technical mode of production, namely, mass society. The comprehensive enveloping of human life by industry and technology has created the technological society, in which technological demands regulate the lives of human beings. The expansion of media has facilitated the process by which technology engulfs human life. As Ellul wrote in his most important book, *The Technological Society* (originally *La Technique: L'enjeu du siècle* [*Technology, The Stake of the Century*]):

> It is the emergence of mass media, which makes possible the use of propaganda techniques on a societal scale. The orchestration of press, radio and television to create a continuous, lasting and total environment renders the influence of propaganda virtually unnoticed precisely because it creates a constant environment. Mass media provides the essential link between the individual and the demands of the technological society.
>
> — Ellul (1964, p. 22)

The four pillars of modern life — technology, society, humanity, and the media — have reached full interaction, both horizontally and vertically, thereby influencing politics, economics, and culture. In so doing, they have gone beyond monopolization and the type of totalitarianism portrayed by the perceptive critic, George Orwell (1949), in his classic book *Nineteen Eighty-four*. The crumbling of the Soviet totalitarian technocracy, however, symbolized the resilience of multiple human nature in resisting one-dimensional and repressive systems. Globalization has helped to form a new community, which is encompassing all of humanity geographically and all aspects of life, including the economy, culture, politics, and even ethics.

69

THE INFORMATION REVOLUTION

In 1973, the sociologist Daniel Bell predicted the coming of what he called "postindustrial society" (Bell 1973). He envisaged humanity's movement from concentration on fabrication and manufacturing to processing, recycling, and services. Interestingly enough, as early as 1951, a Canadian economist and historian, Harold Innis (1894–1952), realized that what was happening went beyond the unfolding of industrial society into postindustrial society. According to Innis, it was communication technology that would affect the future. He began his presidential address to the Royal Society of Canada in 1947 with the following sentence: "Western civilization has been profoundly influenced by communication" (Innis 1951, p. 3). Now, the literature on this concept is blooming and a range of thinkers have written about it. Bell's framework still better explains the nature of this kind of society.

The new information society, according to Bell, has three main features: (1) it involves the change from a commodity-producing to a service society; (2) it concentrates on codification of theoretical knowledge for innovation in technology; and (3) it creates a new "intellectual technology," which serves as a key tool of systems analysis and decision theory (Bell 1979, p. 163). Bell wrote, "when knowledge becomes involved in some systemic form in the applied transformation of resources (through invention or social design), then one can say that knowledge, not labor, is the source of value" (Bell 1979, p. 168). In other words, in this new society, knowledge is the main commodity exchanged in the marketplace. And just as capital and labour constituted the central factors in an industrial society, so do information and knowledge in our own information society.

Canada provides a good example of an information society. Statistics Canada reported that in 1995 the number of employees was 10 673 600, excluding owners or partners of unincorporated businesses and professional practices, the

self-employed, unpaid family workers, individuals working outside of Canada, military personnel, and casual workers. Out of
this number, 8 174 900 people worked in the service industry,
and only 1 675 900 people worked in manufacturing (Statistics
Canada 1997, p. 395). Another telling piece of information is
the use of computers. By "mid-1995, an estimated 3.4 million
Canadians — 17% of the population — were using the Internet"
(Statistics Canada 1997, p. 376).

New thinkers have given up the concept of "postindustrial
society" altogether, because they think it is too vague and it suggests that the new society is a continuation of the past. For
example, the Japanese scholar Masuda wrote, "the information
society will be a new type of human society, completely different
from the present industrial society" (Masuda 1990, p. 3).
Masuda argued that in this new society, the "information utility," that is, a computer-based public infrastructure, replaces
the factory; the "knowledge frontier" becomes the potential
market; the volunteer community replaces private philanthropy
and public enterprises; horizontal social institutions, such as
civil society, replace vertical, centralized public institutions;
and the spirit of "globalism," that is, "a symbiosis in which man
and nature can live together in harmony," replaces "the renaissance spirit of human liberation" (Masuda 1990, pp. 4 and 10).

This kind of optimism is shared by a great number of
people. However, some who accept this basic premise also argue
that the information society has given a central role to the
media, to the detriment of this society. The media set the tone
and define the discourse, and thus it has seemed to many that
the new information society is a vast ocean but not very deep.
Weizenbaum, who was very active in the 1970s in experimenting
and working with artificial intelligence, went as far as to call the
computer revolution "an explosion of nonsense" (Weizenbaum
1976; Postman 1992, p. 116).

Maybe this is the natural conclusion of the industrial mode
of production. Marx observed that "what is called historical evolution depends in general on the fact that the latest form regards

earlier ones as stages in the development of itself" (from the *Contribution to the Critique of Political Economy*, cited in Godelier 1978, p. 250). In other words, no historical epoch is absolutely novel or stands in radical contradistinction to the previous one. Even when Ibn Khaldun used the notion of the "new creation," he meant it to convey the coming of a hitherto unknown challenge, and he then turned to history in search of an appropriate response. The danger of agreeing with Masuda completely is that one's viewpoint becomes ahistorical in the process. Although the information society seems to constitute our future, it has its roots in the past. It makes sense, therefore, to ask about the roots of this new society.

As was suggested at the beginning of this work, an important date for the information society and for civilization was 1989, with the invention of the World Wide Web, comparable in importance to the industrial and agricultural revolutions for industrial and agrarian societies. That date became important because in that year the information mode of thinking, mode of production, and rules of the game came together. But like the previous revolutions, the invention of the World Wide Web had a history proceeding it. It had its roots in a series of events spanning at least two decades. In 1965, the US Department of Defense commissioned the Advanced Research Projects Agency to do research on the "cooperative network of time sharing computers."[22] Soon, in 1969, researchers at four US universities created the first network, the ARPANET, by connecting the universities of Stanford, Utah, and California at Los Angeles and at Santa Barbara. From then on, the network began to grow literally by the minute. In 1973, the ARPANET went international by connecting the American network with University College in London, United Kingdom, and the Royal Establishment in Norway. In 1979, three graduate students in North Carolina established the first USENET newsgroup and opened the net to the ordinary public. In 1986, Case Western Reserve University

---

[22] Not surprisingly, this information is obtained from the World Wide Web, itself.

created the first "freenet" for general public use. The global society was born. Soon, in 1989, Tim Berners-Lee invented the World Wide Web, which is, indeed, the foundation of the global information society. The following year, ARPANET was decommissioned, and the "higher space" became an open-sea, free-for-all.

By 1994, about 50 million people were connected to the Internet, and it is expanding every second. If the medium is the message, then the web is the message of the future (Markoff 1995). A new arena for the actualization of human potential has been born, and if civilizations are the best forum for such actualization, then a new civilization has been born. Unlike previous civilizations, which extended to particular areas of the Earth, the new one covers the globe and has incorporated all of humanity and every civilization.

73

FEATURES OF THE NEW CIVILIZATION

There seems to be a major paradox in the discussion so far, which may appear to be a contradiction. If globalization has produced a new phase of human civilization, why is it claimed that there is one civilization and many civilizations? I shall revert to the definition of civilization presented in the previous chapter for the answer.

Civilization is a condition that allows for a process of concomitant production of political power, economic wealth, cultural values, and even memories. This is the universality of a civilizational milieu. A civilization may at the same time extend to various regions with their own cultural specificity. What is important is that civilizations allow their various components to work out a system of meaning and symbols to provide individual identity and a collective perception of the imagined community — it makes life meaningful for those who participate in it. The agrarian civilizational milieu and its historical systems allowed the Chinese, Egyptians, Indians, and Persians to develop their own systems of meaning while adopting the new agrarian mode of production (cultivation).

This capacity is applicable even to an overriding ideological system as well. For example, the Islamic and agrarian civilizational milieu permitted local and regional systems of collective life. The Abbasids (750–1258) of Baghdad, the Mamluks (1253–1516) of Egypt, and the Moors (711–1492) of Spain were all both Islamic and agrarian, and each dynasty developed its own special mode of civilization production. So it is with the modern industrial mode of production. The Group of Seven countries use the same mode of production (fabrication and manufacturing), and yet each retains its own cultural framework and mores.

Because globalization has made the relationship among its member units very intense and complex, many expect homogenization to follow. If there is any homogenization, it is in the language. English has become the language of the globalized world. Indeed, a recent report of the *New York Times* on the prevalence of English in Europe concluded that

> So strong is the tug of English in Europe that some have suggested it may one day emerge as the continent's universal language, relegating Europe's other languages to the role of regional dialects, in much the same way that languages like Italian, German and even English itself triumphed during the industrialization of the 19th century.
> — Tagliabue (1998, p. 1)

Globalization uses the English language as its medium, but the fact that everyone may speak in English does not mean that the world is homogenized. At one point in Islamic history, almost everyone spoke Arabic and practically all people of the pen wrote in Arabic, but it did not amount to a homogenized civilization. Globalization may be inaugurating a world such as I have termed "one civilization—many civilizations," so well depicted by Gress as follows:

> A fully modern world may have as many, or more, civilizations as did the premodern world because a civilization is not just a matter of democracy, science, and capitalism, but of ritual, manners, literature, pedagogy, family structure, and a particular way of coming to terms

with what Christians call the four last things: death, judgment, heaven and hell. Modernity [read globalization] will not change or remove the human condition, to which each culture provides its own distinct answers.

— Gress (1997, p. 526)

One civilization with the information mode of production (processing and recycling) as its base, encompassing many civilizations, each having its own set of ideas and symbols, constitutes the present human condition. How does one explain this condition? Fukuyama, in the following passage, made a good start in answering this question:

75
→

A society built around information tends to produce more of the two things people value most in a modern democracy — freedom and equality. Freedom of choice has exploded, in everything from cable channels to low-cost shopping outlets to friends met on the Internet. Hierarchies of all sorts, political and corporate, have come under pressure and begun to crumble.

— Fukuyama (1999, p. 55)

I think "freedom and equality" are things that anyone values, whether in modern democracies or other types of regime. To guarantee and safeguard both freedom and equality, one requires a constitutional framework, which, for now, is lacking at the global level. At the practical level, the concept of pluralism captures the main features of the information civilization more accurately, because plurality can exist and even flourish in anarchy, that is, a decentralized and acephalous domain, one without central government. The world is still a domain of self-help where independent states set the agenda and formulate the rules of the game.

A globalized world tolerates plurality in various forms. First, globalization has increased the number of players in the public sphere. In politics, at the international level, there are multiple centres of power, as well as a diversity of actors on the global scene. In the economy, production has become decentralized, making way for multiple producers, with work based on production sharing. In culture, non-Western norms have become important because of the notion of multiculturalism. Second, globalization has shaken the metanarrative of modernity, allowing people to take diverse paths to the truth. It has made it possible to challenge intellectual constructions based on the modern notion of reality. Two important areas in which this is occurring readily come to mind: one is the area of the Western portrayal of non-Western cultural systems and civilizations; and the other is the area of gender and gender relations. Both issues were debated before the advent and flourishing of globalization, but the gender issue has caused the mushrooming of new voices.

Many have challenged Western domination and imperialism, but Edward Said has been the most eloquent and systematic. In his now classic book, *Orientalism* (Said 1978), he showed how a sophisticated, conscious, and sometimes unconscious campaign has created a construction called the "Orient." Orientalism, in Said's words, is "a Western style for dominating, restructuring, and having authority over the Orient" (Said 1978, p. 3). What is important and relevant to our discussion is that Said went beyond partisan condemnation of the West. He showed how not only the notion of "the Orient" but even the notion of the "West," itself, are constructions and imaginary:

> I have begun with the assumption that the Orient is not an inert fact of nature. It is not merely there, just as the Occident itself is not just there either ... . Therefore as much as the West itself, the Orient is an idea that has a history and a tradition of thought, imagery, and vocabulary that has given it reality and presence in and for the West.
>
> — Said (1978, pp. 4–5)

He then gave a detailed presentation of those prominent Western writers who contributed to this construction.

Feminism is the other voice that has challenged Western domination and imperialism. Specifically, it has challenged the double standard involved in affirming the value of both the autonomous, equal, and independent citizen in the political world and the continuation of patriarchal authority in the bourgeois family. This tension lies at the heart of feminist critique, as Lawrence Stone (1979) argued so well in his study of the origin and development of the bourgeois family. How can there be equality and consent in political life and inequality and hierarchy in the family? This is only one aspect of the feminist criticism of the constructed world of modernity. The issue of the public sphere is another.

Benhabib took it upon herself to present an alternative gender-sensitive understanding of the public space, different from that of Hannah Arendt or Jurgen Habermas. Benhabib appreciated Arendt's notions of "civic virtue," or "republican virtue," which so revere action and speech, and Habermas's "discursive public space" in which to restructure capitalist societies to revive democratic socialism. But Benhabib argued that both continue to operate with an exclusive distinction between private and public, inside and outside. "Challenging the distinction of contemporary moral and political discourse, to the extent that they privatize these issues, is central to women's struggles with intent to make these issues 'public'" (Benhabib 1992, p. 110). As Benhabib and other feminists have argued, this is a difficult task because despite the emergence of the women's movement and women's massive entry into the labour force, contemporary political and social theories continue to refuse to adjust to the changing public scene (Landes 1998). They continue to operate with the constructed framework of modernity.

Two points are in order. First, I would not suggest that Said's and the feminists' criticisms of imperialism and modernity are the by-products of globalization; rather, globalization has facilitated the airing of their cause. As suggested above, Nietzsche had already begun an important questioning of modernity and its basic assumptions. A host of Western and non-Western scholars have launched a comprehensive campaign of criticism and sometimes condemnation, but globalization has truly ended history as understood by modernity and its project. Second, although these criticisms have a legitimate and important place in our emerging civilizational conscience, they should not be taken to their extreme. Orientalism in reverse is as bad as Orientalism itself, and female chauvinism is as undesirable as male-based constructions. Cultural milieu and regional communities are aggregates of human beings before they are Orientals or Occidentals, and so on. Individuals are human beings before and above their masculinity or femininity. One never understands this as clearly as when one becomes a parent. You never think of your child in terms of male or female, even if you do not express it, because of the pressure of social preference for one or the other: here, feminists are absolutely right to say that one is conditioned to prefer one to the other. Orientalism in reverse or feminism in reverse is as bad as the constructions these critics are fighting to correct.

Globalization should not be seen as an opportunity for revenge but for a different start. Now that the forces of globalization have provided a *tabula rasa*, one has to be careful not to go to the other extreme. Globalization has not relinquished all restraints and boundaries. For example, it cannot violate the basic rules of logic, ethics, and aspiration, that is, the foundations of the three types of rationality elaborated on in Chapter 2. Instead, it has provided an opportunity for their combined materialization. Many of globalization's rules of the game have emancipatory power and appeal, but one should not take them to be absolutely permissive and anarchic.

POLITICAL PLURALISM, MULTILATERALISM

The Westphalian world recognized sovereignty-bound actors in the public sphere. Globalization has introduced a plurality of actors. Sovereignty is no longer the overriding feature of international relations. Boundaries have lost their traditional meaning. International governance used to mean the collective will of the great powers, expressed in concepts such as "the great game" and "power politics." On Thursday 27 May 1999, the prosecutor of the International Criminal Tribunal for Yugoslavia condemned an active head of a state for violation of the "laws or custom" of war, under Article 18 of the Statute of the Tribunal. This historic and in some ways unusual decision is very significant. The chief war crimes prosecutor, the Canadian judge Louise Arbour, indicted not only the Yugoslav president, Slobodan Milosevic, but also four other members of the ruling elite of Belgrade, with charges of crimes against humanity, especially 340 murders of ethnic Albanian Kosovars, 740 000 deportations, and widespread and systematic persecution. The state no longer has the sanctity it used to enjoy. Standards of proper conduct are not set by states anymore.

Global governance has become too complex for any state alone or even a handful of states to handle. It requires the coordinated efforts of state and nonstate actors. That national and international dialogue among states and organizations is the first step to addressing the newly emerging public challenges was the most important conclusion drawn at a 2-day conference in Ottawa (1–2 October 1998), entitled Policy Research: Creating Linkages, which had the participation of more than 500 academics and practitioners. It is also interesting to note that the treaty banning land mines, signed in Ottawa in December 1997, was the result of a joint effort of the NGOs and the governments of mid-sized powers. The Canadian Foreign Affairs Minister, Lloyd Axworthy, was quite vocal in attributing the success and speed of this process to a "unique coalition of governments, civil society and international groups" (Axworthy and Taylor 1998, p. 190).

Another telling indicator is the evolution of the role of the Security Council of the United Nations. Although it was to operate and be the guardian of the idea of collective security, in practice (to paraphrase Lester Pearson), collective security degenerated into selective security, and the Security Council became the exclusive club of the big powers. During the first four decades of the United Nations, veto power was used about four times each year, whereas in the past decade it has been used only six times. Even the United States feels compelled to legitimize its "imperialistic aspirations" through United

Nations resolutions. As well, the conferences in Rio (1992), Cairo (1994), Beijing (1995), and Kyoto (1997) to deal with development, population, women, and risk-management plans for planet Earth, respectively, displayed multiculturalism at work. However, the massacres in Rwanda in 1996 and in the former Yugoslavia in the past decade, particularly NATO's bombing of Belgrade over the refugee crisis in Kosovo, underscore the limits of multilateralism and the importance of power politics.

ECONOMIC PLURALISM, PRODUCTION SHARING

The postindustrial economic order was already in the making in the 1970s. Economically, the Bretton Woods system, which had preserved the world capitalist system, reached its final phase in 1973.[23] The IMF charter stipulated that the price of the US dollar was fixed in terms of gold (initially at 35 US dollars per ounce) and that all other currencies were to be pegged to the US dollar. Unless a country developed a "fundamental disequilibrium" in its balance of payments (usually interpreted as a "large and persistent" deficit or surplus) and obtained IMF approval to change the pegged value of its currency, the nation would have to maintain the exchange rate through purchases or sales of US dollars, the reserve currency.

The creation of the World Bank and its affiliates to make longer term loans was also considered part of the Bretton Woods system. Shorter term loans were available from the IMF. The

---

[23] The "Bretton Woods system" refers to the post-World War II economic arrangement for saving the world economy. After World War II, the global economy was characterized by high barriers to trade and investment, decimated industries in Europe and Japan, and an exchange-rate system in which the value of currencies was askew. In 1944, some 24 nations met in Bretton Woods, New Hampshire, to map out a postwar strategy to revitalize the global economy. In 1947, an agreement forged the creation of the General Agreement on Tariffs and Trade (GATT), the International Bank for Reconstruction and Development (the World Bank), and the International Monetary Fund (IMF).

destabilizing effects of speculation and persistent US balance-of-payments deficits were seen as the immediate causes of the system's demise in 1973. The US dollar was the key reserve currency, and the United States was reluctant to devalue it, despite persistent deficits. However, countries with surpluses chose to add to their dollar holdings, rather than to revalue. As US deficits persisted, the stock of US dollars held abroad ballooned relative to the need for a reserve currency. Some countries viewed the United States as abusing its privilege of issuing the reserve currency and as forcing other countries to finance its deficits. The eventual increase in the price of gold and the refusal of Germany and Japan to revalue their currencies were the final blows. The fundamental flaw in the system was that it allowed the concern for international liquidity to encourage foreign central banks to hold US dollars. It hindered other nations from revaluing their currencies to eliminate their balance-of-payments surpluses. Ultimately, confidence in the dollar as a reserve currency had to suffer.

Just as the 24 nations meeting in Bretton Woods, New Hampshire, in 1944 had concluded that the post-World War II economy constituted a new creation, so did the world in 1994, on the 50th anniversary of the Bretton Woods system. At that time, it was concluded that a new paradigm was needed to allow a free exchange of currencies at a fixed rate of exchange among the nations. The Group of Seven major industrial democracies, at their Naples summit, decided to consider what framework of institutions would be required to meet the challenges of the 21st century and how to adapt existing institutions and build new institutions to ensure the future prosperity and security of their populations (GSS 1994). The result was the revitalization of what remained of the Bretton Woods system, in the form of the WTO (which has a membership of 133 states, according to the latest count). The delegates at Bretton Woods decided that, in addition to the IMF and the World Bank, an international trade organization should be established as the third pillar of the postwar economic order. A constitution for an international trade organization was drawn up at the Havana Conference, but only Australia and Liberia ratified it, and only the constitution's chapter on GATT was adopted, as a "provisional" measure. WTO was established as part of the final act of the Uruguay Round of GATT, at Marrakech.

I am aware that mainly Western economies originally made these arrangements, making the so-called developing economies simply follow their lead, but one point is well worth noting. As the economies of the newly industrialized countries of Southeast Asia show, when a state is willing and able to take risks and play an active role on the global scene, it can modify the rules of the game, even if it originally did not participate in formulating them. Indeed, all actors of notoriety have demonstrated the dual feature of willingness and ability.[24]

Free trade, removal of barriers, but most important of all, production sharing constitute the new rules of the game in the economic sphere. Production sharing means the internationalization of a manufacturing process, in which several countries participate at the various stages of the fabrication of a specific product. Whereas in the traditional division of labour the core states offer technical know-how and those in the periphery offer raw materials, in production sharing, whoever is prepared to participate in the public sphere of cyberspace is welcome to be part of the producing units. Global production sharing now involves more than $800 billion in trade in manufactured products annually, representing at least 30% of the world's trade in such products. In addition, trade in component parts is growing faster than that in finished products, highlighting the growing interdependence of countries in trade and production (Yeats 1998[25]).

[24] Even God appoints persons of ability and foresight as prophets: all the prophets were well-respected members of their community before they were appointed to their positions. For example, the prophet of Islam, Mohammad Ibn Abdollah (570–632), was a trustworthy and successful merchant before he was appointed to his position.
[25] Yeats, A.J. 1998. Just how big is global production sharing. Paper prepared for the World Bank. World Bank, Washington, DC, USA. Jan.

CULTURAL PLURALISM, MULTICULTURALISM

The term *multiculturalism* invites recognition and celebration of the "others," just as they are, without degenerating into racism in a politically correct guise. In the age of modernity, the key word was *tolerance*. It meant accepting the distinction between "us" and "them" but invited the players "to endure" and "to bear" with their differences. The new age of globalization assumes the validity of all claims to the truth short of absolute relativism. Too much relativism weakens the foundations of any ethical proposition and, with it, the moral foundations of public life. Globalization has made it possible for those who used to be called minorities to have their voices heard. Multiculturalism is thus a paradoxical concept, simultaneously expressing diversity and unity. Globalization involves diversity because it allows for specific expressions of locality and identity, and it involves unity because it promotes the notion of the global village. Without some degree of unity, humanity cannot survive, and without diversity, conformity and lack of fresh outlook will take over. Toleration, thus, gives way to celebration.

Many see multiculturalism as something specific to a given national border. In fact, it is fast expanding into the international domain. As with the new economic order, the quest for a new cultural order has its own history. As suggested above, questioning the universality of modernity's project began more than a century ago with philosophers such as Marx, but it became an important paradigm in about 1980, under the rubric of postmodernism. The age of multiculturalism came with the emergence of the postindustrial information economy, which replaced the previous aristocratic, middle, and working classes with the information elite, the middle class, and the marginalized or underclass. Postmodernism rejects the modernist ideals of rationality, virility, artistic genius, and individualism in favour of being anticapitalist, contemptuous of traditional morality, and committed to radical egalitarianism (see, for example, Docherty 1993).

The effect of this new mode of thinking about the cultural aspects of global civilization is best seen in the area of cultural studies, where appreciative discourse has replaced theories based on real-life cases and specifics and abstractions from them and employs more general structures, that is, ideas of identity. As Grossberg et al. (1992, p. 2) wrote, "cultural studies need to remain open to unexpected, unimagined, even uninvited possibilities. No one can hope to control these developments." The logical consequence of the prevailing tendency in cultural studies is therefore to replace classes with "identities" as the agents of social transformation.

THE GLOBAL PUBLIC SPHERE, THE INTERNET

Aristotle thought that the *polis* provided the best arena for a person to actualize his or her potential. He thought that humanity could survive without the city but that mere survival has never been humanity's ultimate objective. Considering that "the good life is chief end, both for the community as a whole and for each of us individually" (Aristotle 1958, 1278b), humanity has striven toward the establishment of the city because "the end of state is not mere life; it is, rather, a good quality of life" (Aristotle 1958, 1280a). To say what the good life entails would require a separate inquiry, but suffice is to say that the one important component of the good life is that it is meaningful. The meaning has to be articulated in what is today referred to as the public sphere. When one has a good life, one has a strong notion of identity. Modernity constructed this meaningfulness with its three features of universal reason (rationality),[26] national identity (the structure of the nation-state),[27] and industry and capitalism.[28] It was articulated

---

[26] Derrida has dealt with the making of modern utilitarian rationality as the most important modern ideology (Derrida 1982).

[27] The following works show the centrality of nationalism as prevalent identity: Gellner (1983), Hobsbawm (1990), and Anderson (1991).

[28] On the relations between modernity and capitalism, see Derek Sayer (1991).

through the most important means available, the print media, which gradually created an imagined community of cultured members, who read the same books, magazines, and published authorities. In the age of modernity, the "oral tradition" was replaced with the "textual authority." Authors and scholars took over the positions of orators, and the city took the form of the nation-state, comprising sovereignty, people (nation), territory, and defined boundaries.

The citizens of the state were expected to pay allegiance to it in return for its guarantee of the basic rights of life, property, and freedom. Of course, the national arena provides the public sphere for the manifestation of these rights. The new global mode of civilization production, that is, the information revolution, has threatened some of the basic pillars of this constitutional arrangement. Where is the public forum today? Has the new cyberspace formed the new public sphere, which is now at the disposal of anybody who has access to a computer, itself becoming available in traditional public places, such as coffee shops? (It is reported that even in religiously inspired states, such as Iran and Saudi Arabia, new coffee shops with computers connected to the Internet [Internet cafés] have already been established and are growing.)

What, anyway, is the public sphere? Has the growth of NGOs contributed to the growth of a global public sphere? Has the Internet provided a new civil society? Is there a difference between civil society and the public sphere? What is the World Wide Web? The most prominent voice in the treatment of the question of civil society and the public sphere is that of Habermas. For Habermas, the public sphere

> *may be conceived above all as the sphere of private people come together as a public; ... regulated from above against the public authorities themselves, to engage them in a debate over the general rules governing relations in the basically privatized but publicly relevant sphere of commodity exchange and social labour. The medium of this political confrontation was peculiar and without historical precedent: people's public use of their reason.*
>
> — Habermas (1992, p. 27)

This refers to a space in which the powers that be tolerate and respect debate and interaction, but more so, the space in which they accept a critical evaluation of their exercise of power.

The public sphere differs from civil society, however. The public sphere directly concerns the exercise of power and is thus linked to the powers that be, whereas civil society is not directly concerned with power. The public sphere constitutes the realm in which state and society negotiate the boundaries between and among themselves and set the limitations for both citizens and people in authority. Accessibility to the public sphere therefore depends on how much the state tolerates and on the kinds of constitutional guarantees it offers to ensure that such a podium remains at the disposal of citizens and civil-society groups. In other words, whereas civil society defines the sphere of its activities through the initiatives and efforts of its members, the public sphere is at the mercy of the people in authority.

Thus, civil society has always existed, regardless of the form of the state, whether democratic, oligarchic, or authoritarian, but the public sphere flourishes only in open and democratic societies. Indeed, "civil society" refers, in Habermas's language, to the "more or less spontaneously emergent associations, organizations, and movements that, attuned to how societal problems resonate in the private life sphere, distil and transmit such reactions in amplified form to the public sphere" (Habermas 1996, p. 367). He has rightly felt that the public sphere would not have come about without modernity, but this should be qualified by adding that modernity made the notion of the public sphere a general and universal phenomenon through the constitutional and parliamentarian movements of the 19th century and democratization in the 20th century. The Athenians had a public sphere in ancient Greece and the powers that be tolerated it, but it was open only to the citizens, not to the barbarians or slaves. By promoting universal isonomy, constitutional government, human rights, pluralistic democracies, universal franchise, and civil settlement of disputes, modernity has encouraged the emergence of the franchised public sphere.

Has globalization contributed to further growth of this phenomenon or has it weakened or destroyed it? The answer to this question is paradoxical. The World Wide Web has surely helped the growth of civil societies. It has become the new public sphere, although for some it is only a virtual public sphere. It is growing enormously. The Clever Project of the IBM Almaden Research Center in San Jose, California, claimed, in *Scientific American*, that "everyday the World Wide Web grows by roughly a million electronic pages, adding to the hundreds of millions already on-line" (MCP 1999, p. 54). As "textual authority" loses its credence, the print community is being replaced with the "virtual community" and the "virtual public sphere," in which people from all over the world debate and comment on all issues, including the very meaning of life. By enlarging the domain of the debate and by allowing more participants into it, the World Wide Web has contributed to the enhancement of freedom (by creating more choices and empowering people to make these choices) and equality.

Will this new pluralism, the mushrooming of global players, the multiplication of the rules of the game, and the assertion of multiple cultural voices lead to a more collaborative world or to a world of discord and competition? On the surface, identity politics has become the most prominent feature of the contemporary world, to the point that, to recall the 1970s feminist slogan, even "the personal is political." But in reality, it seems that the notion of "the political" is being distorted. To politicize an issue is one thing; to look at it politically because politics is part of our very existence is quite something else. As Jean Bethke Elshtain rightly suggested,

> *Being political is different from being directly and blatantly politicized — being made to serve interests and ends imposed by militant groups, whether in the name of heightened racial awareness, true biblical morality, androgyny, therapeutic self-esteem, or all the other sorts of enthusiasms in which we are currently awash.*
>
> — Elshtain (1995, p. 81)

87

"Being political" gives rise to responsible civility, whereas "being politicized" leads to extremism. Globalization has the potential to do either. As we will see, some argue that it has led to a radicalization of "the political," construed through such notions as the clash of civilizations, a subject discussed in the next section.

CLASH OR DIALOGUE OF CIVILIZATIONS

Those who define the terms of the debate not only set the tone of, but also shape, the discourse. Historically, on the eve of any new creation, one hears both the forecasters of doom and gloom and the prophets of optimism and light. In 1798, Thomas Robert Malthus wrote a best-selling pamphlet on population. Based on the premise that populations grow far more quickly than food supplies, the pamphlet predicted that the United Kingdom would soon face starvation. That set the tone and defined the discourse for a long time, although the author was proven wrong. In the same period, the French revolutionaries presented a different discourse, that of "liberty, equality and fraternity," which helped humanity in its fight against the injustices of oligarchy, autocracy, plutocracy, totalitarianism, and tyranny. The French revolutionaries also declared the right of the ordinary people to take part in the public life of their homeland as citizens, rather than mere subjects, setting in motion what Gasset (1960, p. 91) later called the "revolt of the masses." Both paradigms have remained with us in the forms of the conservative and revolutionary traditions, and both have helped us balance our lives in the face of challenges.

What about now? As argued above, humanity is facing another new creation. Similar reactions have appeared. Huntington predicted pessimistically that the future of human civilization is replete with the clashes of civilizations. He rests his paradigm on five assumptions:

- ➤ "It is human to hate," hence the ubiquity of conflict (Huntington 1996, p. 130);

-❧ The "other" in the form of tribe, race, and civilization, is the source of insecurity;

-❧ People's quest for domination over others and for control of territory, wealth, and resources remains the sources of conflict; and

-❧ Socioeconomic modernization of the individual has created alienation and dislocation, thus creating the need for social identities; and

-❧ Individuals have multiple identities, which may reinforce or contradict one another.

I will not go into a critical evaluation of these assumptions but say only that the first presupposes a Hobbesian world in which people are ready to stab each other, whereas the others involve a cultural-determinist view of human nature. Both human emotion and cultural categories are time and place bound. They require careful investigation.

Huntington (1996, p. 91) presents a historicist account of the encounters of civilizations as nothing but competition and clash: "The distribution of cultures in the world reflects the distribution of power. Trade may or may not follow the flag, but culture almost always follows power." As "the West will remain the most powerful civilization well into the early decades of the twenty first century" (Huntington 1996, p. 90), the natural conclusion would be that the world should conform to the American way of life. Because some people insist on their local cultural identity, a clash of civilizations is inevitable.

However, many prominent scholars have thought differently about this new phase in human history. Long before the current debate on the clash of civilizations, Habermas (1987, p. 296) declared that "the paradigm of the philosophy of consciousness is exhausted" and urged us to shift to "a paradigm of mutual understanding." The key concept lies in the last phrase, particularly the notion of "mutual." It presupposes that it takes two to have a relationship, "we" and the "other." A new paradigm of mutual understanding does not mean the elimination of the "other." This would be logically and realistically impossible. Attempts to assimilate native children into the prevalent "white Christian" culture in North America resulted in tragic alienation, deracination, and cleavages. The irony is that, had the experience succeeded and had all natives been assimilated, I do not think it would have resulted in the enhancement of human culture but the formation of the homogenized corporate individuals, so graphically portrayed in Orwell's (1949) *Nineteen Eighty-four*. Such societies, if ever possible, are the ultimate manifestation of domination — in this instance, of a particular form of life and mode of rationality.

In a society free of hegemony and domination, diversity of opinion and versatility are natural. Here lies the important distinction made in Persian political culture between two objectives of public life: one is *jahangiri*, best translated as "conquest" or "empire"; and the other is *jahandari*, or "statecraft, administration, and civilization." The paradigm of the clash of civilizations leads to conquest. Note the great clashes instigated by Alexander the Great, Genghis Khan, Napoleon, the West in its encounter with the natives in the new continent and in the world over, and the worst one, that of Hitler. Their most important achievements have been conquest, tragedy, and historical scars. Dialogue, in contrast, leads to interaction and learning that result in mutual growth and the creation of civilization. It allows for the growth of the multiple dimensions of humanity and the actualization of all its potentials, as identified in Chapter 2, which, in the end, leads to *jahandari*. *Jahandari* and *jahangiri* are related, because a civilization needs *jahangiri* to establish its core state, define its own world, and make its presence known, but if it remains in that mode, it is bound to fail. The experience of the Soviet Union is still fresh in everyone's mind. It adopted a hegemonic mode for more than half century, and it remained an empire without ever achieving any civilization.

Another example is the venture of Islam and the Muslims' interaction with other civilizations. The first two centuries of Islamic history constituted an era of clash and consequently of domination and conquest, whereas in the next two centuries, it was an era of dialogue. Islamic civilization learned from the Greeks, the Persians, and the Romans. The strategy for dialogue had two components. One was the formulation of a curriculum, which included learning from the "other," and the other complementary component of this strategy was the "House of Wisdom" (Dar al-Hikma). As Makdisi (1990, p. 88) remarked, "in classical Islam, knowledge was organized into three major divisions: (1) the Arabic literary arts, (2) the Islamic religious sciences, and (3) the 'foreign sciences' or 'the sciences of the Ancients', especially the Greeks." The House of Wisdom was established to facilitate the study of "foreign sciences." Again, as Makdisi remarked,

> The movement of Greek books from Byzantium to Baghdad began in earnest with a letter from Caliph al-Ma'mun [ruled 813–833] to the Byzantine sovereign. ... The books chosen and brought back gave impetus to the translation movement begun by the Caliph's father Harun ar-Rashid [ruled 786–809], and eventually brought about the Arabic–Islamic explosion of knowledge.
> — Makdisi (1990, p. 81)

The end result of this interesting dialogue was not only a learning process of the first order but also, in the long run, a further glorification of both Islam and the Hellenistic heritage. The example of Islam and the "foreign sciences" is typical. One could apply that to the story of the Greek, Japanese, Roman, Western, or many other civilizations.

Indeed, the notion of a clash of civilizations is a contradiction in term. If there is civilization, it will avoid clash. Clash leads to conquest and empire and indeed the destruction of civilization. Historically, civilizations have learned from each other while each stays unique. As Braudel observed (1994, p. 178), "the history of civilizations ... is the history of continual mutual borrowings over many centuries, despite which each civilization has kept its own original character." The difficult task is to formulate a device to include the "other." In the fall of 1997, the prominent historian, William Hardy McNeill, ended the text of his lecture "America and the Idea of the West" with the following:

> *So insofar as a concept of the West excludes the rest of humanity it is a false and dangerous model. Situating the West within the totality of humankind is the way to go, and we should in our classrooms move as best we can in that direction, believing always in the ennobling effect of enlarging one's circle of sympathies, understanding, and knowledge, and aspiring to share that belief with our students. There can be no higher calling for historians, and above all, for teachers of history.*
> — McNeill (1997, p. 524)

An important component of this calling is the realization that our global village will not survive if we do not learn to live together and break the barriers that our particular imagined communities have created around us. What is positive about globalization is that it has made the notion of living together easier.

Am I assuming that the global village will have no notion of the "other" or even have the thought or wish that it should have no such notion? Not at all. Common sense dictates that as long as the notion of the unknown remains alive in humanity, it will have a notion of the "other." My plea is for the recognition that the "other" may, in many ways, be an asset rather than a liability or the source of insecurity and danger.

The next chapter elaborates on this point. Here it is enough to say that the appeal for the recognition of diversity has strong religious, moral, and even secular grounds. From the viewpoint of religion, we are all creatures of one God, the lord of here and hereafter. From the viewpoint of morality, our one world reminds us that the social ecology and natural environment can stand only so much exploitation. Secular rationality cautions us that any harm afflicting one part of the world has a direct bearing on every other. We should remind ourselves of the words of the Iranian sage Sheikh Moslehadin Sa'di

(1213–1293), which are, interestingly enough, engraved on the wall of the main building of the United Nations:

> *All Adam's children are members of the same frame:*
> *Since all, at first from the same essence came.*
> *When by hard fortune one limb is oppressed:*
> *The other members lose their wonted rest.*
> *If thou feel'st not for others' misery:*
> *A child of Adam is no name for thee.*
>
> — Sa'di (1979, p. 38)

The new global civilization has brought challenges, dangers, and opportunities. It has greatly facilitated interactions among people, but it is not a panacea. Similar to other historical epochs, it has its own heterogeneity and contradictions. Gramsci's important observation applies to globalization. He wrote, "A given socio-historical moment is never homogeneous; on the contrary, it is rich in contradictions" (Gramsci 1985, p. 93). Globalization, has, however, modified our priorities, demands, and responses. Old ways no longer suffice. This topic will be dealt with in the next chapter.

93

The Future of Global Governance

The history of man is a graveyard of great cultures that came to catastrophic ends because of their incapacity for planned, rational, voluntary reaction to challenge.
— Erich Fromm (1968, p. 62)

So far, I have refrained from making any judgment about the consequences of globalization. It was a conscious decision on my part. I wanted to be able to stand back and present a comprehensive picture of what is taking place on the global scene. The preceding chapters have shown that globalization simultaneously affects the economic, political, social, and religious realms. Precisely for this reason, globalization presents many challenges, some of which are positive and some of which are negative. I deal with these challenges in this chapter.

Globalization has, indeed, produced a "global village," a result of modern communications, as postulated by the Canadian thinker, Marshall McLuhan (1989). Globalization has not, however, resulted in a global political identity that fosters global loyalty and solidarity. Nationalism is still a very powerful ideology and demands loyalty from a country's citizens and entails a responsibility for the security and welfare of their polities. Loyalty and reward thus form the two sides of the same coin. A similar duality of "international citizenship" and "international polity" has not yet been created to form the two sides of a valid and valuable international coin. Instead, globalization has given rise to ethnic nationalism, identity politics, and unfortunately, in many cases, tribalism of the worst kind. The following examples immediately come to mind: the Taliban in Afghanistan, the Serbs in Bosnia and Kosovo, and the Hutu in Rwanda.

Globalization operates as a two-edged sword. It emancipates but also represses, and it brings together and unites but also divides and forms new hierarchies. It encourages mass participation in the economic world. It likes to see individuals acting as aggressive players and participants in this world to keep the consumer market economy flourishing. Stephen Gill reported in 1995 that "today about 70 percent of US families have at least one credit card, up from 50 percent in 1970" (Gill 1995, p. 23). Right after Khomeini's death, in 1989, when the neoliberal economy was emerging in Iran, VISA and MasterCard signs appeared on the windows of major commercial and financial institutions in Tehran and other large Iranian cities. At that time, I sarcastically commented to the managers and executives about the coming of "the Great Economic Satan." The shopkeepers responded by invoking globalization and its power to facilitate their participation in the international economic system.

In the areas of culture and politics, however, the role of globalization is not very clear. At one level, it advocates passive consumption of cultural products and prefers to turn individuals into loyal spectators of the political status quo. At another level, it enables individuals and groups to voice their cultural and political grievances by providing them with more efficient and accessible modes of communication. Then again, at one level globalization makes individuals and groups aware of the peculiarity of their local setting by exposing them to others in their own living rooms and making them more global by bringing to their attention broader loyalties and their membership in the community of the one planet Earth. This paradoxical nature of globalization was captured by the sociologist Roland Robertson (1992, p. 102): "We may best consider contemporary globalization in its most general sense as a form of institutionalization of the two-fold process involving the universalization of particularism and the particularization of universalism." Globalization introduces many universal commodities, values, and rules of the game that were once particular to one area or another, but they will not be accepted in other places if they disrupt the regional cohesion too drastically.

Two examples are important to note. One is the coming of modernity to the Middle East, and the other is the sexual revolution in America. Constitutional movements need to set up legislative assemblies, individual rights, and the electoral process, parts of the modernity project. Middle Eastern countries did not find it difficult to adopt legislative assemblies, because this notion could be localized under that of consultative bodies, which had historically existed in the region, whereas adopting the other two parts of the modernity project proved much harder — the struggle to secure human rights still continues. In America, although the so-called sexual revolution has been occurring for decades, the predominance of the puritanical tradition has not allowed it to change modes of behaviour as radically as in Europe, particularly in Scandinavian countries. This global–local interaction is perhaps the most interesting challenge of globalization, and it has generated a variety of responses. Just as an example, it threatens our identity — once so connected to the state — provides us with a broader identity, if we understand it and adjust our thinking to it.

CHALLENGES

What are the challenges of globalization for our understanding of the human condition as it pertains to global governance? As shown above, globalization has affected all spheres of human existence — political, economic, cultural, and social — and requires new ways of doing and thinking. As a new phase in the human civilizational process, globalization has presented a comprehensive set of challenges to the established order. Here, I deal with some of these under two headings: theoretical and practical challenges.

THEORETICAL CHALLENGES

The greatest theoretical challenge of globalization is, ironically, its success in creating an interconnected world. It has brought the "others" physically closer to one another. A United Nations document claims that there are 10 000 distinct societies living in more than 200 states (UNESCO 1995). Globalization has connected them, brought them into regular contact, and made them dependent on one another. Globalization has resulted in the creation of an "association" of humankind but not a "community," to use the important distinction that the sociologist F. Tonnies (1955) drew some years ago. For example, I leave my home to go to work every morning. Next to me lives someone very different from me. He is from another country and culture, has a different background, lives a different life style, and even wears different clothes from mine. His thought processes and aspirations differ from mine. We are so close and yet so far apart. The "other" has come as close to me as my doorstep. Politically correct behaviour demands that I pretend that I do not see the difference. But do I know anything about that life style?

The degree to which diversity surrounds us today was unimaginable two decades or even one decade ago. Political scientist Karl Deutsch (1966, 1988) suggested that if the peoples of the world interacted more, they would make it possible to form a more cohesive international community. Such interactions would lead to a "we feeling" among communities. As a result, the governments would become committed to the peaceful resolution of international disputes. According to Deutsch, this "we feeling" would enable humanity to unlearn the system of national exclusion emphasized by nationalism and the attitude of absolute loyalty to the state. He even contemplated the formation of a "security community," where sovereign states would feel confident enough to trust their national security to a multilateral arrangement (Deutsch 1957). If cooperation is conceivable in the most sensitive areas of international politics, then there is hope for its occurring in other spheres. Globalization has created a "community" in the sense that the various segments of humanity live close together, but it has not brought them closer to a peaceful world. Possibly, the underlying problem is the persistence of the old notion of the "other." The most important challenge, therefore, is to formulate a theory to include the "other" without completely assimilating the "other" into one set of ideas and practices.

How does the existing theory of the "other" differ from the traditional theory of the "other"? By the "traditional theory", I mean that based on the pre-Renaissance cosmological worldview, founded on religious communal solidarity. It operated on the assumption that all humanity belonged to the same family, all children of Adam, although some of its members had gone astray. As Toynbee and Caplan wrote,

> In recognizing that the under-dog, too, has a religion of a kind, albeit one that is erroneous and perverse, the top-dog is implicitly admitting that the under-dog is after all, a human soul; and this means that the gulf fixed is not a permanently impassable one when the distinction between sheep and goats has been drawn in terms of religious practice and belief.
> — Toynbee and Caplan (1972, p. 430)

The pre-Renaissance worldview contained little sense of superiority—inferiority or difference in kind between people. If it had distinctions, they were a matter of degree and could be removed through conversion and attainment of excellence. In contrast, the modern theory of the "other" is based either on racial and ethnic hierarchy, as developed by thinkers like Herbert Spencer (1820–1903), or on the politics of exclusion, in accordance with the notion of *raison d'État* (Meineche 1957). The modern theory of the "other" creates a strong caste system that is impossible to penetrate. The attitude of modern imperialist conquerors of foreign lands toward the natives, branded as "the spawn of inferior races" (Toynbee and Caplan 1972, p. 436), is an important historical example.

The irony is that modern secular societies have achieved a good deal of respect for human dignity, albeit more so at the national than at the international level. This was accomplished through the notion of tolerance, supported and guaranteed by a powerful legal system. To paraphrase a famous Roman saying, all roads lead to the social contract, in the form of a national constitution. In other words, turning everyone into a "citizen" solved the problem of the "other." Such a conversion would be more difficult to accomplish at the global level. We have no global constitution, and there is no accepted legal system to apply to an anarchical international system that still sees virtue in the dominant role of the sovereign state.

PRACTICAL CHALLENGES

The first and most comprehensive practical challenge of globalization stems from its tendency to undermine all boundaries and encourage people to express any position and develop any product that the market can absorb. The explosion of video games and ridiculous games on the Internet that anyone can play and that imitate life experiences are cases in point. They encourage the lowest common denominator and the worst mediocrity. The political philosopher, Leo Strauss (1958), commented that Machiavelli had found it so difficult to attain virtue as defined by the classic traditions and philosophers that he redefined it in terms of skill, mundane achievement, and secular excellence. Many see globalization as doing the same thing and even as exaggerating the process. In *Jihad vs. McWorld*, Benjamin Barber (1995) critically examined the effect of globalization. "McWorld," he wrote, "is a product of popular culture driven by expansionist commerce" (Barber 1995, p. 17). Globalization has made popular culture accessible to everyone to the point that it has become a virtual reality controlled by "invisible but omnipotent hightech information networks" (Barber 1995, p. 26). Jihad is a form of jealous "dogmatic and violent particularism of a kind known to Christians no less than Muslims, to Germans and Hindus as well as to Arabs" (Barber 1995, p. 9). In short, globalization has brought two extreme sides of humanity to the surface, both of which are detrimental to human dignity. As Barber wrote,

> *Neither Jihad nor McWorld promises a remotely democratic future. On the contrary, the consequences of the dialectical interaction between them suggest new and startling forms of inadvertent tyranny that range from an invisibly constraining consumerism to an all too palpable barbarism.*
> — Barber (1995, p. 220)

Although this is a very exaggerated conclusion, it points to a paradox of two seemingly opposite human characteristics. On the one side is extreme consumerism, or what Herbert Marcuse (1964, p. 3) used to call the totalitarian tendency of the market, which operates "through the manipulation of needs by vested interests." On the other side is extreme demagogy, totally manipulating human emotion and psychology for exclusive aims. In the case of McWorld, the persuasive and seductive forces of the market incapacitate human reasoning; in the case of jihad, blind obedience to a particular interpretation of dogma suppresses the power of reason. Practical solutions are needed to enable a more moderate dimension to manifest itself in the globalization process.

A second practical challenge of globalization stems from its deconstruction of many familiar institutions by questioning their very foundations, thus creating institutional vacuums. The most radical of these deconstructions is that of the authority of the state as the final arbiter for citizens, which has occurred to such an extent that many talk about the end of the state. This process actually began when the Russians launched the first satellite from the Baikonur cosmodrome in Kazakhstan on 4 October 1957. The implications of this occurrence were made vividly clear to me in 1993, when I was driving with a diplomatic correspondent through Iran. He asked me to stop in the middle of nowhere to allow him to contact his editor. When I mentioned that we had to drive for another hour to reach a telephone, he surprised me with his satellite phone. He set it up quickly and made his contact. The absolute, indivisible, and comprehensive sovereignty of the state, as French political philosopher Jean Bodin (1530–96) defined it, crumbled before my very eyes. All or most of the modern political, economic, and social idols fell into the twilight zone (Wriston 1992). The sovereign state provided identity, based on an imagined community where intersubjective communication took place. It provided the means of socialization through symbols, ceremonies, national anthems, celebration, and education. Above all, it provided a public sphere where social and political accountability, responsibility, and duties played themselves out. Now the question is, Where does one's loyalty lie? What is the source of one's identity? We need to take practical political and legal steps, such as recognition of dual and even triple citizenship, to help individuals cope with the coming of multiple identities.

Although globalization has not ended the importance of the states themselves, it has made state borders less important. It has influenced the extent of the states' power and has given rise to an interesting practical problem, the fate of the marginalized or failed states and communities (Buzan 1991; Ayoob 1995). Even here the impact of globalization is paradoxical. It has made powerful states more powerful and made weak states weaker and more fragile. Statistics speak more clearly. Between 1989 and 1996, there were 96 armed conflicts in the world, 91 of which were intrastate conflicts and nearly all of which occurred in developing countries. According to the Stockholm International Peace Research Institute's 1996 yearbook (SIPRI 1996), all major armed conflicts in 1995 were internal. Is this the result of globalization? The answer is yes, to a certain extent. The political scientist Fred Riggs (1964, 1973) argued that many developing societies have lost their internal cohesion as a result of their encounter with modernity. Indeed, the introduction of modernity into these societies acted as a prism, reorienting them and turning them into a state neither traditional nor modern. Globalization's comprehensive nature has exacerbated this inherent weakness. At the same time, globalization has created its own class, a "cosmocracy," and thereby marginalized a good portion of the middle class in these societies. Some national communities have thus become centres of internal strife and have, as a result, been marginalized. Is the solution to restore the state? Has globalization the potential to do this?

The vanishing or weakening of borders is not limited to physical or geographical boundaries. The conservative writer William Gairdner (1998, p. 65) edited a collection of essays in search of "freedom, virtue, and order." The authors lamented the weakening of the family, parliamentary democracy, educational systems, media, and welfare states — institutions expected to provide peace, order, and good government. These institutions have fallen victim to the deconstructed, globalized world. The authors argued that the new mode of thinking encourages the worst forms of radical individualism. Such individualism ignores the inherent tensions between the organic demands of the community — particularly its nucleus unit, the family — and the impulses of the atomized person (Gairdner 1998). We are facing crises of authority in the family, community, and religious establishments, a crisis of power (in that our traditional understanding of power relations no longer holds), and a crisis of values (in that everything is considered relative). In short, globalization has discredited all forms of hierarchy.

The combined result of these theoretical and practical challenges is that we no longer feel we are in charge. Our central bank cannot set the value of our currency. Our central government cannot protect our security. No longer is our family the refuge we used to turn to. Our governance has become synonymous with global issues. What should our responses be?

RESPONSES

Every new creation tends to deconstruct many of the familiar existing institutions, mores, and practices and replace them with new ones. A new creation invites us to forgo the familiar and adopt the unknown — a very disheartening challenge, indeed. How does one respond to such a threatening situation?

TYPOLOGY OF RESPONSES

Arnold Toynbee identified two extreme positions in people's responses to any new challenge: those of the Zealots and those of the Herodians. These two concepts grew out of the Jewish reaction to Hellenism in the first half of the 2nd century BCE. The Zealots were those who rejected the Greek civilization, and the Herodians were the supporters and admirers of the Idumaean king, Herod the Great, who advocated borrowing every one of the Greeks accomplishments. The Zealots felt they should keep their own indigenous customs, rather than allowing the new civilization to define their identity. These viewpoints are not opposites but two sides of the same coin: both responses "are in practice desperately defensive attempts to ignore or forestall a new situation produced by the introduction of a novel dynamic element into the life of a society" (Toynbee and Caplan 1972, p. 442).

Overwhelming approval of or stubborn refusal to accept any phenomenon leads to radical reactions: the first demands absolute conformity, and the second expects absolute denial. These are recurrent extremes in modern history. After the industrial revolution, humanity demonstrated the same kinds of reaction. The best examples of denial are the Luddites and the Amish, and the best examples of conformity are the secular reformers of the non-Western world, like Mustafa Kemal Ataturk (1881–1938) in Turkey and Reza Khan Pahlavi (1877–1944) in Iran, who advocated the imitation of Western civilization at a time when members of the traditional religious class were advocating complete detachment from it.

Perhaps the most famous uprising against modern industry was the Luddite movement in the United Kingdom. The Luddites were named after their leader, "King" Ludd, or Ned Ludd. They organized against technological advances in the textile industry during the Regency era, from 1811 to 1816. They thought these advances were threatening their way of life and livelihood. The revolt ended when Parliament dispatched 12 000 soldiers, and the leaders of the movement were either executed or deported to Australia. Another example is that of the Amish people in the United States, who have quietly resisted modern industry and lived according to a concept of "submission—yielding" to a higher authority — God, the church, elders, parents, community, or tradition, but not the secular modern state. Their creed demands obedience, humility, submission, thrift, and simplicity. In the view of the Amish, faith and tradition should permeate every aspect of social practice. For example, telephone service, which was introduced into Lancaster County, Pennsylvania, in 1879, was officially banned in the Amish community in 1909. The Amish continue to reject modern technology, today, and live a simple life, but they are not active in their opposition.

Ataturk and Reza Khan advocated a wholesale imitation of industrialization. One important protagonist of Herodianism in the region coined the phrase "Westernization from head to toe" (Taqizadeh 1920, p. 1). A massive project of reform from above was implemented in both Iran and Turkey, and the social fabric of each country was disrupted enormously as a result. In the case of Iran, this process sparked a revolution with the aim "return to the self," as projected by revolutionary activists like the sociologist Ali Shariati (1982). The traditional Muslims responded by advocating complete abandonment of industry and modernity, thereby contributing greatly to a resurgence of religious fundamentalism after modernization and secularism proved ineffective.

Globalization has generated similar extreme reactions. The so-called computer nerds feel that the solutions to all our problems will be found in the new information technologies, whereas active and radical opposition groups and individuals feel that globalization has caused the degeneration of social and cultural life. The most famous case of individual opposition to globalization is that of the "Unabomber," whose manifesto was a rejection of everything modern or technological. Indeed, he began by saying that "the Industrial Revolution and its consequences have been a disaster for the human race ... . The continued development of technology will worsen the situation" (introduction, www.unabombertrial.com/manifesto/index.html). To give an example of group opposition, one can point to the followers of the radical right, both in the West and in other parts of the world. That segment of the Islamic movement that advocates exclusivity and follows a policy of eliminating the "other" is as bad as its counterpart in the West that advocates "social cohesion" by limiting immigration and thereby eliminating the "other." The Taliban in Afghanistan are ready to use the most modern arms to re-create and preserve the most traditional and tribal form of society!

Attitudes of exhilaration and immutability correspond to overconfidence and insecurity, respectively. Whereas the former encourages unquestioning approval, the latter encourages a nostalgic return to the past, radical fundamentalism, and too much inward looking, intolerance, and insularity. I suggest a third possible attitude — prudent vigilance. It recognizes the negative and positive consequences of globalization and the fact that nothing is constant. Yet, it also recognizes the need to link humanity to both the past and the future and to see continuity and change as two pillars of human existence.

This third alternative occurred to me in 1986, when I felt a moral obligation to return to my native homeland of Iran to teach. On seeing my determination, Kenneth W. Thompson, the international relations theorist, wished me luck but wanted me to remember prudence and vigilance. Iran was in the midst of one of the bloodiest and longest conventional wars in the 20th century (1980–88, with more than 1 million dead and injured on both sides). Also, I dove into a postrevolutionary situation in which the revolution was still unfolding and occasionally devouring its own children. Although it was not easy, a combination of vigilance and prudence guaranteed my survival. It might in part be a good recipe for survival in the information and technological revolutions. But vigilance and prudence cannot by themselves be enough, because they only help us to avoid errors and to ward off possible dangers. Creative initiative is also needed to guarantee worldly and secular, as well as spiritual and moral, enhancement. Surprisingly, the best method to achieve these goals is what has been with humanity all along, that is, using common sense.[29]

The common-sense response recognizes that globalization is not homogenization, conformity, or following someone else's project but a process of becoming one globe, in terms not only of physical interconnectedness but also of moving toward a global human community of diverse societies. Common sense recognizes that modernity and the modernization project have created great impediments to realizing such a community. A notable aspect of this legacy is the following dual process: on the one hand, modernization has alienated humanity from all its roots — family, land, clan, and tradition — by making everyone an uprooted, atomized bourgeois individual; on the other hand, it has demanded absolute loyalty to the official faith of the state, that is, nationalism. Despite such impediments, the common-sense response is to see the new phase in human civilization as an invitation to try out new ideas, approaches, and methods. Common sense tells us that more moderation is appearing in the radical movements of the past couple of decades, that is, Islamic revivalism in the Muslim world, evangelical Christian fundamentalism around the world, Hindu revivalism in India, and the Judaic one in Israel. I am aware that radical groups still display Messianic zeal on the eve of the new millennium, and this may dampen optimism. However, great

---

[29] In an important book, Garnet shows the virtue of this method in international politics (Garnett 1984).

opportunities lie ahead. It is possible to identify areas needing radical change, others needing modification, and still others needing preservation. But one has to be guided by the profound prayer, "Oh, Lord give me the courage to change those things that I can change, the patience to accept those things that I cannot change, and the wisdom to know the difference." Not surprisingly, I first saw this insightful benediction in a work of political philosophy (Spragens 1976, pp. 53–54).

What are some of these areas? The common-sense response is that the main task should be to achieve sustainable civilization production, using an appropriate theoretical framework, creative institutions, and comprehensive mechanisms and rules of the game. The ultimate objective, we must remind ourselves, is to minimize human suffering and anarchy and to establish a just order. Order without justice leads to tyranny, and justice without order dissipates into chaos. For example, globalization has not only weakened physical borders but also reduced the moral significance of national boundaries. On the surface, this is a simple statement. However, from the standpoint of the Westphalian system of states, based on territory and fixed boundaries, it heralds the weakening of one of the most important institutions of modern times, namely, the state.

States used to create order, both nationally and internationally, although it was not always a just order. The centrality of the state and its monopoly over the use of violence, as Weber defined it, have been the symbols of injustice for many. Now, states are no longer the only actors. Many feel that the weakening of state power has unleashed a new tyranny, world economic capitalism. The state used to maintain a balance between political and economic forces. It also used to guarantee some degree of distributive justice. Capitalism is only concerned with maximizing interest and increasing capital gains. But now the capitalist system has reached its peak. As John Kenneth Galbraith commented, in a CBC interview on his 90th birthday, on 14 October 1998, if the capitalist economy is left unchecked it will bring about another disaster, worse than the one experienced in the 1930s. Our response to globalization, therefore, has to be both comprehensive and well thought out and has to address its theoretical and practical challenges.

THEORETICAL RESPONSES

The most important theoretical response should be to formulate a new framework for understanding the "other" that would combine the local and the universal. It should include everyone while making each feel that his or her uniqueness is recognized and appreciated. How does one accomplish this difficult task?

An understanding of the notion of the "other" is an important starting point. Samuel Johnson (1709–84) once remarked that in a civilized society we all depend on each other. The concepts of "each" and "other" can make important contributions to sustaining civilization and making it endure and flourish. The key task is to define these concepts. For a long time, humanity perceived its various segments as various worlds, unaffected by each other. In our one world, they have become not only interdependent and mutually inclusive but also, I dare say, one and the same in the physical sense, but the notion of the "other" has remained. The fact remains that the notion of the "other" has been with humanity and will remain. The "others" include civilizational milieus taken not only synchronically but also diachronically; they exist across geographical borders and through time.

The British historian of civilizations, Arnold Toynbee (1934), identified more than 20 civilizations as the "others." Although extensive cross-civilizational fertilization has taken place, only recently have these civilizations become so closely interconnected. Thus, never before have we had such an urgent need to live in tranquillity with, and in appreciation of, each other's achievements. Did past civilizations have any notion of the "other"? Yes, but not in the same way as we understand this today. Up to the time of the Renaissance, human history was thought to operate within a sacred cosmological order, in which everyone, including the "other," was part of the bigger order of being. But, who is the "other"?

It has been argued that the destruction of the cosmological world order, which gave birth to the Cartesian "I," or the modern person, also gave rise to an exclusionary notion of the "other" (Nasr 1981). Although the ancient world had some notion of the "other," it did not brand that segment of the populace as irrational, primitive, or marginalized. The moment the "others" welcomed and accepted the dominant belief system, this automatically removed their "otherness," and they were included as members of the community. The postmodernist thinker Michel Foucault (1926–84) spent a lifetime on what he termed the technology of the self, to understand the ways the West has developed knowledge of the self. He concentrated on the internal "others," such as the mad person, the deviant, the prisoner, the delinquent, and the murderer. The literary theorist Edward Said (1978, 1993) has focused on the construction of the "other" internationally in his two works, *Orientalism* and *Culture and Imperialism*. Both Said (1965) and Foucault (1977) claimed that the notion of the "other" is a construct used to manipulate people for the sake of power.

Uprooted from tradition, family ties, nature, and metaphysics, acting only on the predominant Machiavellian system of thinking, the Cartesian "I" appeared on the Earth to dominate it. No wonder knowledge is defined as power and promotes the notion that "might makes right." The modern "I" sees history as a way of dominating the past, sociology and politics as ways of dominating fellow beings, and technology as a way of dominating nature. One has to prove that one is the fittest in order to survive in the constant struggle for existence. The paradigm shift to modernity did not change the nature of human beings; rather, it changed humanity's priorities. History informs us of the otherness in other epochs, but this otherness was different from that of the age of modernity.

How different was it? First and foremost, there was a holistic understanding of the mundane world and the creatures in it. In this cosmological worldview, the world was considered an organic creation, in which, in the language of Muslim philosopher—mystic Mahmud Shabestari (*d.* 1320), "if one small parcel was removed from it the totality of its order, the world will fall apart." This philosophical and ontological understanding of humanity had its social and legal manifestation in a hierarchical system that defined people's privileges and obligations in terms of their social status. Thus, *Pax Romana* was based on a strong Roman legal system comprising *jus civile* and *jus gentium*, and the *Pax Islamica* was based on the Islamic legal system (the *shari'a*), with its distinct rules and regulations for Muslims and the other "peoples of the book," that is, followers of other monotheistic religions. Nevertheless, an inclusive feature of all these systems was that they would not allow for the occurrence of such phenomena as the Armenian genocide, the Kurdish refugees, the Holocaust, apartheid, Palestinian refugees, and ethnic cleansing in Yugoslavia, Rwanda, Albania, and Kosovo, so prevalent in the 20th century. No record of similar occurrences can be found in human history before the age of modernity. The atomized individual of the post-Renaissance era is responsible for the exclusionary approach to the understanding and construction of the human condition reflected in these events.

The "other" has been defined in two ways. One defines it in terms of a collective in which the core members of the prevalent historical system have one set of rights and responsibilities and the "others" have their own. The other defines it in terms of the framework of modernity and stigmatizes those who are not players in the modernity project. The modern understanding of the "other" was much more exclusionary than the premodern one. Now, considering the fact that the notion of otherness has always been with humanity and globalization has made one glob of the various civilizational components of the human commonwealth, how can one formulate a framework in which "us" and "them" are replaced with "both"?

The first step in developing a future alternative would be to diagnose the source of the notion of otherness. One may consider two possible sources of this notion. One is the fear of the unknown. The following story, which I heard from a wise man of my village a long time ago, left a lasting impression on me. It went as follows: Someone was arrested for treason in the middle of a desert. He was brought before the chief of his tribe and given the option of suicide by a pistol or facing whatever was waiting for him behind a black curtain. The man shot himself because he feared the unknown behind the black curtain. On examination, it turns out that the curtain was hung over a door that opened to the street and to freedom.

Another possible source of the notion of otherness is the fact that the "other" appears to us as our mirror image, showing us what we really are, without hiding it in sweet talk and pleasant images. It presents an honest picture of us. The feeling of the unknown, the naked, or the critical is unpleasant. "When the mirror reflects who or what you are, do not break the mirror, re-examine yourself," explains a Persian verse. But as the life and death of Socrates demonstrated, self-examination, questioning, and being fearless in the face of the unknown can be a hazardous enterprise. It is always much easier to blame the other, break the mirror, or poison Socrates.

There is a hopeful sign, however. Humanity has revered and remembered Socrates precisely for his daring ventures in questioning the unknown and teaching us that "an unexamined life in not worth living." The unknown, therefore, has not always been seen as a source of danger but sometimes as a constructive challenge to our minds. The two protagonists of the global scene — namely, "the West" and "the rest" — are each the other's unknown and mirror image. However, each can turn the other into a source of strength, rather than a threat. Remember the adage, "nothing ventured, nothing gained"! The great minds responsible for discoveries, inventions, explorations, contemplation, and even revelations left us great legacies precisely because they ventured into the unknown and moved beyond the world of the familiar.

What should we do with the "other"? I have already alluded to the political scientist, Abraham Kaplan, who distinguished between internal and reconstructed logic as two ways of understanding a phenomenon. The former takes us to the heart of any subject under consideration, whereas the latter refers to a construction on our part. Internal logic is a "cognition directed to understand the subject matter under study, whereas reconstructed logic is 'in effect, a hypothesis'" (Kaplan 1964, p. 8). This distinction is crucial to understanding and developing our attitude toward the "other." One can either get into the internal logic of a phenomenon or construct one for it and call it knowledge. As Edward Said (1978) documented in his now classic *Orientalism*, so far Western scholars, writers, and travelers have constructed an imaginary understanding of the East because they consider the people of that region the "other." Recently, the "other," particularly the Islamic world, has been presented as the new menace in world politics. These days, the catch phrase is "the Islamic threat" (Esposito 1992; Halliday 1996). The predictions of clash and doom exaggerate the degree to which humanity can decide on which position or course of action to take.

One can either take the path of constructing a short-sighted and self-serving picture of the "other" for the end purpose of domination and conquest or take a long-term view and understand the internal logic of the "other" for civilization production and sustained social and communal life. The latter approach requires some important changes in one's perception of, and attitude toward, the "other" and the recognition that the barriers need to be deconstructed. The President of Mali, Alpha Ouma Konaré, expressed similar feelings in 1993:

> As long as any civilization applies political, intellectual and moral
> coercion on others on the basis of the endowments that nature and
> history have bequeathed to it, there can be no hope of peace for

humanity: the negation of the cultural specificities of any people is
tantamount to the negation of its dignity.
— Cited in (UNESCO 1995, p. 53)

Scholars such as David Held (1996) have contemplated the
theory of inclusion, which avoids negating any cultural specificity, and they have made calls to build an international community and create international citizenship guaranteed by a
system of cosmopolitan democracy. A theory of international
community has been developed by Andrew Linklater, for
example, an international relations theorist. His is concerned
with the study of political community, and he thinks that modern attempts to build a political community have failed because
modernity's conception of universal morality is "hostile to cultural differences" and because "the monopoly of powers at the
disposal of sovereign states" has hindered the materialization of
"societal potentials" (Linklater 1998, pp. 27–28). He has further suggested, *à la* Habermas, that humanity has come to a new
juncture in its moral standards. Linklater wrote,

> *There are three main stages of moral understanding: the pre-*
> *conventional, conventional and post-conventional. At the level of*
> *pre-conventional morality, subjects obey norms fearing that non-*
> *compliance will lead to sanctions imposed by a higher authority; at the*
> *level of conventional morality, they obey norms from a sense of loyalty*
> *to existing social groups or peers; at the level of post-conventional*
> *morality, subjects stand back from authority structures and group*
> *loyalties and ask whether they are complying with principles which*
> *have universal validity.*
> — Linklater (1998, p. 91)

The main and important component of postconventional
morality is the notion of universal citizenship based on the
moral equality of persons. It is universal, fair, and inclusive.
"Sound reasons have to be offered for treating individuals differently" (Linklater 1998, p. 57). Such morality will lead to the
transformation of the present political community with the aid
of "dialogic" communities, "which are cosmopolitan in orien-
tation, respectful of cultural differences, and committed to

reducing social and economic inequalities, nationally and internationally" (Linklater 1998, p. 109).

Linklater offers important insights, but he seems to be too idealistic in thinking that the nation-state system will change any time soon. He hopes for the transformation of the prevalent complex world system, a hope that seems to border on the realm of the impossible. I believe that the state, as the accepted form of organization for a fragmented humanity, will remain relevant. The economist J. Helliwell demonstrated, in his new book (1998), that the widely held belief that globalization has resulted in international economic linkages that are as strong as those within nations is dramatically mistaken. The historian Eric Hobsbawm (1996) argued that the state will remain relevant to our political life for the near future and that the idea of a world government or even a federation of states will remain wishful thinking for the foreseeable future.

How does one formulate a theory of the "other" that is inclusive and yet preserves the distinctive features of the various components? In 1991, the United Nations and the United Nations Educational, Scientific and Cultural Organization (UNESCO) established the World Commission for Culture and Development, under the presidency of Javier Perez de Cuellar, the former Secretary General of the United Nations. UNESCO brought on board many prominent scholars and practitioners. Its report may help us here. As the report suggests, an international government is possible if we can formulate a "global ethics" that encompasses humanity the world over:

> It is part of the fundamental moral teachings of each of the great traditions that one should treat others as one would want to be treated oneself. Some version of this "Golden Rule" finds explicit expression in Confucianism, Taoism, Hinduism, Buddhism, Zoroastrianism, Judaism, Christianity and Islam, and is implicit in the practices of other faiths. The deeply human urge to avoid avoidable suffering and some notion of the basic moral equality of all human beings together form an indispensable point of reference and a strong pillar of support for any attempt to work out a global ethics.
>
> — UNESCO (1995, p. 36)

The inclusive theory of the "other" would invite us to consider humanity as one family, one community of vulnerable souls. The overworked motto "understanding makes a world of difference" should be invoked once more.

An all-embracing theory of the "other" must begin with understanding, but with understanding what? I shall go back to the notion of a complex, integrative approach suggesting a holistic view of humanity, discussed in Chapter 1. To begin with, it was shown that human beings are simultaneously religious, political, economic, and social. The powerful tendencies of individualism and communitarianism go side by side. Human beings need to have their individual spaces to feel that their individuality is materialized but need the community for that individualism to be recognized. This paradox shows how human beings need others, but without being invaded by them. There is plenty of each, but not very much of both. As a person of both the East and the West, I am always struck by the fact that in the West my sense of individuality feasts, whereas my sense of community and affinity with others starves, and in the East I am faced with the opposite condition. This dual impulse may make it possible to develop a theory of the "other" that advocates unity in diversity. At the national level, it has been done with the help of the notion of pluralism. Unity within plurality under a common legal system has made this dream a reality. Now, globalization has altered the distinction between the national and the international domains. Looking "inside out" is an option. The international scene is not as anarchic (Bull 1995) as one used to think, and the national one is not as orderly as one used to assume (Walker 1993).

There is an important question to consider here. Do the interactions of the existing "others" constitute a battle of worldviews or the battle of ideas? It appears that the first state of affairs results in a zero-sum game among the adherents of those worldviews, whereas the battle of ideas may contribute to fruitful interactions, which may in turn lead to the "dialogic communities" Linklater wished for. Until the Cold War, it was assumed that a battle of worldviews dominated world politics and that it would result in the annihilation of humanity. John Foster Dulles, the US Secretary of State in the 1950s, accused the members of the Non-Aligned Movement of supporting the wrong side in the war between good and evil, by not taking sides. And, of course, the West was on the side of the good. To cast the post-Cold War era in the same terms, as Huntington seems to be doing, would bring worse consequences than those experienced during the Cold War. What makes us human is our ability to tolerate those with a different worldview than our own and appreciate those with different ideas. The appreciation of different ideas is at the heart of civilizational cross-fertilization.

The battle of worldviews may lead to war only within a given closed community, whereas at the level of an international system of states, it may present a challenging mirror for self-examination. Globalization presents an agenda requiring both a battle of worldviews and a battle of ideas. A battle of worldviews is occurring now between a good portion of humanity that has recognized the evil of inhumane attitudes and practices and those who still believe in exploitation and hang on to the constructed notions of the superiority of this or that group or class. But even here, as the removal of Suharto from power in Indonesia showed, the battle of worldviews is leading to positive consequences — in this instance, the exposure of injustices and corruption.

A comprehensive theory of the "other" takes the complex integrative approach as its foundation, along with an organic view of the various forces within each human being, in place of the compartmentalized outlook. It tolerates those who hold completely different worldviews and celebrates those with different ideas.

PRACTICAL RESPONSES

Many of the responses to the practical issues of globalization require new *modi operandi* if they are to be successful in solving some of these new global issues. Two of these issues seem to be most pressing. One is the need for new institutions, and the other is the need for new rules of the game. One of the challenges of globalization concerns the crisis of authority of the old institutions. They no longer command the same legitimacy. As the international theorist I.L. Claude (1986) reminded us, it was states that formed and managed the existing international institutions (that is, international governmental organizations) and set the functions of these institutions. This was true when states were the only actors at the global level. What about now, given the current pluralism of actors?

Bridging institutions

Emerging new players and the pluralistic nature of the international scene require a new kind of institution to act as a bridge between states, individuals, and global civil society. What form should the new institution take? How can such institutions serve many masters at the same time? The experience of the European Union is enlightening and provides many of the answers to such questions, but with one important reservation. The European Union is the commonwealth of Europe, and its members have historically shared many cultural and societal norms and mores. The important prerequisite for the creation of a form of social cohesion was already in place. Can a similar experience be repeated at the global level?

The following debate between two political scientists is highly instructive. A few years ago Adda Bozeman (1971) saw little hope for the future of international law as a set of common rules of the game for nations. In response, James Piscatori (1986) documented how Muslim countries were quite comfortable in playing by the international rules of the game, despite the cultural differences between Muslim and secular modern states. Since that debate many events — such as the 1979 anderolepsia in Iran (during which American diplomats spent 444 days in captivity) — have confirmed Bozeman's pessimism, whereas the Iraqi invasion of Kuwait supported Piscatori's argument (important Muslim countries came to the aid of the allied forces to punish Iraq for violating an important principle of modern international law, namely, the sanctity of borders) (Piscatori 1991).

David Held, professor of politics and sociology at the Open University in the United Kingdom, has argued that it is possible to create bridging institutions. He based his argument on the concept of "cosmopolitan democracy," which he defined as "broad avenues of civic participation in decision-making at regional and global levels" (Held 1996, p. 354). He proposed a bridging institution to connect the new emerging players on the global scene with the still significant traditional players, such as nation-states:

> The case for cosmopolitan democracy is the case for the creation of new political institutions which would coexist with the system of states but which would override states in clearly defined spheres of activity where those activities have demonstrable transnational and international consequences.
>
> — Held (1996, p. 354; see also 1995, chap. 10)

New rules of the game

A strong message of the Ottawa conference (GCON 1998) on public policy was the notion that linkages should be created not only between various institutions at the national level but also between national and international players. One needs to consider international dimensions in making even national decisions. Governance entails a complex decision-making process, in which national and international aspects have become extremely interdependent. Moreover, groups and individuals that have become international actors are now putting pressure on traditional international law, which mostly addresses relations among nations.

A few years ago, the philosopher John Rawls (1993) suggested that "the law of peoples" should be devised to regulate relations between various communities. This was an extension of his idea of justice as fairness, which he had presented in his much-debated book, *A Theory of Justice* (Rawls 1971), about two decades earlier. The law of peoples is based on a measure of tolerance. As declared in the charter of the International Court of Justice, the sources of traditional public international law are treaties, customs, principles of law held by civilized people, and the opinions of prominent international jurists. The last two sources have an obvious Eurocentric tone and content. Rawls used the notion of the law of peoples in an attempt to modify that. He began with the following question: "What form does the toleration of nonliberal societies take?" Then he continued,

> *Surely tyrannical and dictatorial regimes cannot be accepted as members in good standing in a reasonable society of peoples. But equally not all regimes can be reasonably required to be liberal; otherwise, the law of peoples itself would not express liberalism's own principle of toleration for other reasonable ways of ordering society nor further its attempt to find a shared basis of agreement among reasonable peoples.*
> — Rawls (1993, p. 37)

Rawls recognized three types of society: liberal, hierarchical, and tyrannical. Only the third should not be tolerated, because tyrannical regimes fail to respect the minimum conditions for global governance, which rest on respect for human rights.

However, Rawls did not deal with the philosophical basis of global human rights in this essay, although he dealt with the more general issue elsewhere (Rawls 1971). For the philosophical basis of global human rights, we have to turn to the German humanist thinker, Hans Kung (1990, 1994, 1996), who has devoted his life to promoting the notion of global ethics. At the base of this new ethics is the acceptance of what Kung called *humanitas*, or true humanity.[30] This seemed to Kung so significant that he concluded that even the credibility of religion

---

[30] Kung presented this idea in one of UNESCO's meetings. See Kung (1990).

depends on how far it promotes human dignity. The new rules of the game are not, therefore, based on the prevalent principles of "the civilized world," but on how much the new rules contribute to upholding the very essence of a human being.

What therefore constitutes the rights and duties of the individual in a globalized information society? The European Commission devised certain rules for it, based on a "shared vision and common principles," one of which is as follows:

> Access to information is a basic right for every citizen. The information infrastructure will be vitally important for social and economic interaction and integration. The benefits of the information society should not be limited to business but should be available to society as a whole. Social cohesion both in a national context as well as on a world scale requires that all citizens, wherever they live, can benefit from essential information services at an affordable price.

New vernacular

Those who define the terms of discourse set the agenda for the future. In January 1998, the newly elected President of Iran, Muhammad Khatami, gave an exclusive interview to the Cable Network News (CNN). Among other things, Khatami said that mistrust had dominated relations between Iran and the United States. He was referring to US–Iranian relations since the revolution. The United States broke diplomatic relations with Iran in 1980. Iran had been calling the United States "the Great Satan," and the latter had been calling Iran "the rogue state." With Khatami's interview, a 20-year discourse of animosity changed overnight.

Another example of the power of a change in discourse is found in the language of hostility between the Western and the Soviet blocs in post-World War II global politics. It began when Winston Churchill made his memorable speech at Westminster College in Fulton, Missouri, on 5 March 1946, after receiving an honorary degree. The most famous line was the following: "From Stettin in the Baltic to Trieste in the Adriatic an iron curtain has descended across the Continent" (Churchill 1946, p. 7290). The phrase "the Iron Curtain" described the division between the Western powers and the Soviet Union. This discourse was inspired by a policy of containment, as conceived by the American statesman George Kennan (1947). Containment then constituted the main vernacular of East–West relations. Nikita Khrushchev proposed the principle of "peaceful coexistence," which not only changed the discourse of politics but also profoundly affected practical policy decisions.

An appropriate discourse is also required for the global age. A new mode of reasoning is needed to set the tone for a dialogue of civilizations. Such dialogue requires a new theory of the "other," a new mode of thought, and a new *modus operandi*.

Unexplored issues

A number of other issues are worth mentioning. The first concerns the future role of the media. The media have traditionally been thought of as a mere means of communication. However, they have become important actors on the global scene. For example, CNN has become a powerful international institution. What is the consequence of this important event for global governance? Does this new role change the function of the media in the political arena?

The second issue relates to the effect of globalization on the educational system. What type of education is relevant to the new generation? A student in an advanced society was asked where fruits come from, and the student's response was that they came from a can. What kind of response would one get from someone of a generation whose world is shaped by the virtual reality of multimedia? What is the impact of the information society on education? What do we mean by "world history"? The immediate response of educational institutions to the information revolution has been to computerize the schools. I personally doubt that more gadgets can ensure the quality of education needed for the new generation.

A third issue concerns the internationalization of crime. The weakening of state boundaries and the emergence of non-state actors has encouraged criminal activity at the global level.

One may argue that there is nothing novel about this. There have been historical cases of outlaws being important political actors. For example, Braudel remarked that the pirates were important global actors in the age of Phillip II (1527–98), the King of Spain (Braudel 1972). However, in the age of international law, democratization, and global governance, one expects that international crime would now be under control. In reality, though, it has intensified. Human smuggling and money laundering are two examples of the growth of global crime, which has grown to such an extent that the 1994 Naples Summit of the Group of Seven countries declared the following: "We are alarmed by the growth of organized transnational crime, including money laundering, and by the use of illicit proceeds to take control of legitimate business. This is a world-wide problem with countries in transition increasingly targeted by criminal organizations" (GSS 1994). Indeed, we are now faced with a computerized Mafia. This seems to be a contradiction: How can the underground survive in the information age, for which transparency and an open society are the prime requisites?

A fourth issue concerns the changing nature of traditional political and international concepts. It has been suggested that the nature of power has changed. Now, soft power is much more important than traditional military and armaments. Does *power* mean the same thing as it used to? How does one define *security*? Who is responsible for order if states decline or fall into the twilight?

A fifth issue relates to the remarkable speed with which the middle class is shrinking. The numbers of the very rich and the very poor have increased in the past two decades. The industrial mode of production was extremely labour intensive and relied on a great many bureaucrats, technocrats, and industrial workers, thus generating a vibrant middle class. The information mode of production is intellect intensive, needing only a small cosmocracy. The main effect has been the radicalization of the public domain and the coming of an age of extremism. Just as an example, the labour force is being sharply divided between people who are information-technology literate and receive enormous salaries, incomparable to traditional middle-class incomes, and those who are not. More important than the big salary gap is the fact that the loyalty of the information-technology cosmocracy lies not within the local community or even the state, but with an abstract corporation that moves these people around the globe. This is changing the nature of political debate by giving precedence to partisan politics over national politics. How can this trend be modified? Is it inevitable?

A sixth issue, which according to many is very urgent, is that of the environment. Our mode of exploitation of the resources of the Earth has endangered the biosphere. It is like "sitting on the branch and cutting down the trunk," as the Eastern wisdom puts it. How do we strike a balance with nature, so as to use it but not to abuse it?

A seventh issue concerns demographic change. First, the population of the world has reached a high of 6 billion and is expected to reach about 7 billion by 2010 and 8.2 billion by 2025. Second, the world's elderly population is growing. Whereas overall population growth stands at about 1.5% a year, the population of people more than 65 years of age is increasing at an annual rate of 2.7%. Then there is the disparity between population increases in industrial countries and those in the poor regions. The industrial countries have very low fertility rates, and the median age of their populations has risen to close to 40 years, whereas populations of the poor regions are getting younger and younger. Moreover, the severe shrinkage of the extended family in one area and its rapid growth in another may create an imbalanced quality of population. How will this affect global governance?

These are only a handful of issues I mention in passing. Others directly affect the future of global governance. Combined with yet other issues and trends that I have outlined above, these issues point to the observation with which I started this work, namely, that humanity is facing a new creation, which is complex, overwhelming, comprehensive, and inclusive. To quote political philosopher Tom Darby,

> As a civilization, the West has made its choices, and in going global has reached the end of its journey. The paths that lead to planetary conquest were justified by Christianity, by the "white man's burden," and then by Westernization, "modernization," "development," and now by "globalization"; each more abstract than its predecessor, hence more inclusive. But humanity has begun an adventure, and when an adventure begins, there is no turning back.
>
> — Darby (1996, p. 23)

Our new adventure involves all of humanity, with the consequence that there is no longer any hegemonic power at the helm. The state, defined as the only actor on the world scene, has many contenders, from NGOs to civil societies and individuals. Now the question to consider is who should take responsibility for global governance.

The politics of global civilization, if it is to deliver global governance, may begin with the assumption that all members of the human race are citizens of the emerging one civilization — many civilizations. This does not mean equality, or equal status for all. This would be homogenization in its extreme form, which is neither desirable nor sustainable. Distinction is the hallmark of human society. The equal society of sameness would be a boring place to live, and I think nobody would care to inhabit it. *Equality* rather means that the global civilization should operate with isonomy, that is, with equal accessibility to both negative freedoms (lack of restraints on one's exercise of free will) and positive freedoms (availability of the means to actualize one's potential) (Berlin 1958). The first implies freedom from intrusion, harassment, and discrimination — in short, any form of exclusion. The second implies the availability of the means and opportunity for human elevation.

Although Berlin (1990) felt that human integrity is threatened in societies in which massive social engineering is used to achieve a utopian world in the name of positive freedom (1990), the new human civilization requires some degree of responsible social engineering. But this should not be conducted

by a particular state or organization; rather, it should be conducted by each individual based on his or her means and
prospects. For example, Charles, Prince of Wales has engaged in
organic farming to counteract the soulless legacy of the 1950s
and 1960s, the peak of the age of progress and industrialization
everywhere. At the time, interestingly enough, the Club of
Rome published its report reminding humanity of the limits of
progress (Meadows 1972). It is up to each individual to act as a
responsible citizen of the world.

CHAPTER 5

Conclusion

As the overworked French expression suggests, "the more things change, the more they stay the same." No doubt, the globalization process has produced the new creation, which is bound to modify our perceptions of time and space, but I doubt that it has altered humanity's nature, anxieties, or predicament. Nor do I think that the new creation of the global age, the global village, or the World Wide Web has marked the end of history or produced the last man. Arnold Toynbee rightly remarked that constant challenge and response are the hallmarks of the human saga. Globalization has presented a new challenge and requires a new response.

The challenge of this new creation seems to be somewhat different from that of previous ones, owing to its universality: it involves all of humanity, either actively or passively, and it theoretically and practically affects all spheres of politics, economics, culture, and even religion. Why is this different from the challenges of industrialization and its associated narrative of Westernization, which were also universal and comprehensive? Unlike the modernity project, globalization does not claim to possess the truth. Postmodernist discourse has presented a corrective to the monopoly of objective, scientific, and verified truth. Thinkers such as the political philosopher Tom Darby (1982) and the literary theorist and social critic Edward Said (1993) have rightly pointed out that in the modernity project, the realms of know-how and technology, theory and practice, came dangerously close together. Knowledge was at the service of power, rather than truth. People of the pen were agents of particular interests, rather than lovers of wisdom, and universities became vocational institutions, rather than places of human excellence or, in Platonic language, of conversion, where human beings changed direction and directed their minds toward the truth. If there is an end to history, it is this understanding of it that has come to a close.

In the modernity project, history was reduced to just that phase of the human saga during which modernity and industrialization joined forces to produce a new era in the life of the human community and brought the paradox of "everything solid melting into thin air." Science, with its "unlimited progress in the 'conquest of nature'" (Strauss 1959, p. 93), was expected to secure the hegemonic rule of "developed" humanity over both nature and other people. After having melted the world in which the cosmological worldview of divine and natural order held sway, modernity's solution for securing political order was power and *security*, defined in terms of power. Globalization and the alliance of information processing and postmodernist thinking not only melted but evaporated the constructions of the modern human being, whom Hobbes (1968 [1651], p. 81), in his introduction to the *Leviathan*, referred to as having "greater stature and strength than the Natural." The "social contracts" embedded in national constitutions and the anarchical "international system" of states crumbled at end of the 20th century.

Way before it became fashionable, Tom Darby (1982, pp. 158–170) talked about the end of this history and attributed it to the emergence of the "universal and homogenized state." On Darby's reading, modernity and, to some extent, globalization have produced such homogenization. I feel, though, that what turned modernity into a homogenizing force was the "Western narrative" of modernity and, in turn, Westernization, which took, for a while, the form of Europeanization and later became Americanization. During the 1960s and 1970s, under the rubric of development, the United States began to advocate economic reform from above, as by "an enlightened dictator," to solve the ills of the Third World. Iran was considered the most successful case of this nature, but, as is well documented in Halliday's *Iran: Dictatorship and Development* (Halliday 1979), that country was not modernizing, nor was her leader, Muhammad Reza Pahlavi (ruled 1941–79), enlightened. Indeed, the program of economic reform paved the way for the Islamic revolution and the establishment of an Islamic state. That is why many see globalization as the Americanization of the world economy and of global culture, through multinational corporations and Hollywood, respectively.

As the previous chapters have shown, globalization is much more than a project. It is a sophisticated process that requires a new way of doing and thinking. Even if it began as a project, it changed completely: 1989 truly marked "the end of history" according to the Western narrative of modernity and inaugurated the beginning of a new era, whose main features are still taking shape. In the previous chapters, I talked about some of these features, based on some rather clear signs: pluralism, an open society, a universal public sphere, and the legitimacy of multiple narratives are the components of the new phenomenon of one civilization — many civilizations. The revolt of the masses has come through a complete circle. The actualization of the power of the ordinary masses, in the form of NGOs at the international level and of civil society at the national level, is striking. I will just stay with the example of Iran. Lobbying efforts of NGOs at the United Nations led to resolutions calling for human rights in Iran and for regular monitoring of its policies on minorities, but it was active political support and civil society that brought the reformist and moderate president Mohammad Khatami to power, marking the Thermidor of the Islamic revolution (Rajaee 1999).[31]

---

[31] *Thermidor* refers to the 11th month of the French Revolutionary calendar. After the *coup d'État* of 9 Thermidor (27 July 1794) overthrew Robespierre and ended the Reign of Terror, the group that assumed power became known as the Thermidorians. They removed economic controls, thus unleashing inflation, and established some freedom of worship. The term *Thermidor* is now used to signify the end of any revolutionary era.

Globalization has not homogenized the world, nor has its universalization affected everyone in the same fashion. Indeed, it is not surprising that the perceptive economist, Samir Amin (1966), thinks that the defining characteristics of globalization are its reinforcement of the unequal distribution of wealth between various parts of the world and its promotion of a growing disparity between the developed and developing countries and regions of the world. However, it seems to me that from time immemorial, every human organization has displayed a hierarchical order, with various groups or individual members having distinct statuses and particular privileges. No human aggregate gives total equality to its members. Isonomy — that is, equality before the law — is one thing, but being equal in all respects is something quite different.

The challenge of the new creation is to find a new way of thinking about globalization and formulating priorities. The holistic, integrative paradigm of restoration is intended to provide just that way of thinking, with pluralism, dialogue, celebration of the other, civility, global responsibility, and constant learning as its main components. This last notion, that of learning, as understood by the political philosopher, Michael Oakeshott, is the key to unlocking the secret of the new creation. For Oakeshott, "learning is not merely acquiring information ... nor is it merely 'improving one's mind'; it is learning to recognize some specific invitations to encounter particular adventures in human self-understanding" (Oakeshott 1989, p. 29). Adopting this way of looking at the new framework for understanding globalization is all the more imperative at the threshold of the new millennium, when the human condition is so precarious.

Globalization has empowered many and disempowered many others. The empowered should not submit to the politics of conformity, and the disempowered should not resort to the politics of resentment. To follow one's particular interest in the name of the demands of the individual or to withdraw from the public sphere would both be damaging to long-term civilization production. I feel that both responses would fit Elshtain's (1995, p. 74) conception of "individualism," as distinct from "individuality." Global individuality should replace global individualism. Conformist individualism fails to see the opportunities provided by globalization — as a historical *tabula rasa* — and resentful individualism fails to recognize the challenges of the new creation. Globalization is a road neither to utopia nor to disaster; rather, it is a new epoch, with its own peculiarities and challenges, calling on humanity to respond to these challenges. As past experience has shown, any new adventure entails both fear and hope. Globalization similarly provides opportunities and presents dangers. It helps us to discover the unknown by opening new horizons. But it also threatens to shake the foundations of our known world. It is up to humanity to act responsively and proactively. It is also important to consider the depiction of life in the verses of the contemporary Iranian poet, Siyavash Kasra'i:

> *O yes, O yes, life is beautiful*
> *Life is but an old fireplace*
> *If you light the fire*
> *The dance of its flame will be seen from far away*
> *And if not, it will be dark*
> *For which only you should be blamed.*
>
> — Kasra'i (1999, p. 70
> [author's translation
> from the Persian])

Bibliography

REFERENCES CITED

Amin, S. 1996. The challenge of globalization. Review of International Political Economy, 3(2), 216–259.

Anderson, B. 1991. Imagined communities: reflections on the origins and spread of nationalism. Verso, London, UK.

Arendt, H. 1951. The origins of totalitarianism. Harcourt, Brace and World, New York, NY, USA.

———— 1958. The human condition. The University of Chicago Press, Chicago, IL, USA.

———— 1963. On revolution. Viking Press, New York, NY, USA.

———— 1970. On violence. Harcourt, Brace and World, New York, NY, USA.

Aristotle. 1958. The politics of Aristotle (edited and translated by E. Barker). Oxford University Press, Oxford, UK.

———— 1979. The Nicomachean ethics (translated by W.D. Ross) (18th printing). Oxford University Press, Oxford, UK.

Axworthy, L.; Taylor, S. 1998. A ban for all seasons: the Landmines Convention and its implications for Canadian diplomacy. International Journal, 53(2), 189–203.

Ayoob, M. 1995. The Third World security predicament: state making, regional conflict, and the international system. Lynne Rienner Publishers, Boulder, CO, USA.

Ayoub, M. 1999. Encounter of cultures, Islam, a religious pluralism. Paper presented at the Islam and the Challenge of the New Millennium conference, 9–10 Apr, McGill University, Montréal, PQ, Canada. Institute of Islamic Studies, McGill University, Montréal, PQ, Canada.

Bannan, T.S. 1988. Ibn-Taymiyyah's theory of political legitimacy. University of Nebraska, Lincoln, NE, USA. PhD thesis.

Barber, B.R. 1995. Jihad vs. McWorld. Times Books, New York, NY, USA.

Bell, D. 1966. The end of ideology: upon the exhaustion of political ideas in the fifties (rev. ed.). Free Press, New York, NY, USA.

———— 1973. The coming of post-industrial society. Basic Books, New York, NY, USA.

———— 1979. The social framework of the information society. In Dertouzos, M.L.; Mosesin, J., ed., The computer age: a twenty-year view. MIT Press, Cambridge, MA, USA. pp. 163–211.

Benhabib, S. 1992. Situating the self: gender, community and postmodernism in contemporary ethics. Routledge, Chapman and Hall, Inc., London, UK.

Berlin, I. 1958. Two concepts of liberty: an inaugural lecture delivered before the University of Oxford, on 31 October 1958. Clarendon, Oxford, UK.

———— 1990. The crooked timber of humanity: chapters in the history of ideas. Murray, London, UK.

Bernstein, R.J., ed. 1985. Habermas and modernity. MIT Press, Cambridge, MA, USA.

Bienenstock, R.; Homer-Dixon, T. 1998. The end of pop economics. Globe and Mail, 3 Sep, p. A21.

Bozeman, A.B. 1971. The future of law in a multicultural world. Princeton University Press, Princeton, NJ, USA.

Braudel, F. 1972. The Mediterranean and the Mediterranean world in the age of Phillip II (translated by S. Reynolds). Vol. 1. Harper and Row Publishers, New York, NY, USA.

———— 1973. Capitalism and material life, 1400–1800. Harper and Row Publishers, New York, NY, USA.

———— 1980. The history of civilizations: the past explains the present. In Braudel, F., ed., On history. The University of Chicago Press, Chicago, IL, USA. pp. 177–218.

———— 1994. The history of civilizations. Penguin Books, London, UK.

Bull, H. 1995. The anarchical society: a study of order in world politics (2nd ed.). Columbia University Press, New York, NY, USA.

Burger, P.L. 1996. Secularism in retreat. The National Interest, 46 (Winter), 3–12.

Bush, G. 1991. Public papers of the presidents of the United States, 1990. Vol. 2. United States Government Printing Office, Washington, DC, USA.

Buzan, B. 1991. People, states and fear: an agenda for international security studies in the post-Cold War era (2nd ed.). Lynne Rienner Publishers, Boulder, CO, USA.

Carrasco, D.; Swanberg, J.M. 1985. Waiting for dawn: Mircea Eliade in perspective. Westview Press, Boulder, CO, USA.

Churchill, W. 1946. The sinews of peace, 5 March 1946. In James, R.R., ed., Winston S. Churchill, his complete speeches, 1897–1963. Vol. 7. Chelsea House Publishers, New York, NY, USA. pp. 7285–7293.

Claude, I.L., Jr. 1986. The record of international organizations in the twentieth century. Tamkang University, Taipei, Taiwan.

Coate, R.A.; Alger, C.F.; Lipschutz, R.D. 1996. The United Nations and civil society — creative partnerships for sustainable development. Alternatives, 21(1), 93–122.

Cox, R.W. 1992. Towards a post-hegemonic conceptualization of world order: reflections on the relevancy of Ibn Khaldun. In Rosenau, J.N.; Czempiel, E.O., ed., Governance without government: order and change in world politics. Cambridge University Press, Cambridge, UK. pp. 132–159.

———— 1995. Civilizations: encounters and transformations. Studies in Political Economy, 47 (Summer), 7–31.

Dahrendorf, R. 1959. Class and class conflict in industrial society. Stanford University Press, Stanford, CA, USA.

Darby, T.W. 1982. The feast: meditations on politics and time. The University of Toronto Press, Toronto, ON, Canada.

———— ed. 1986. Sojourns in the New World: reflection on technology. Carleton University Press, Ottawa, ON, Canada.

———— 1996. Globalization, resistance and the new politics. The Literary Review of Canada, 6(9), 3–8.

———— 1998a. On globalization: 1st essay, the right to rule the planet. Kritika and Kontext, 2, 8–19.

———— 1998b. On globalization: 2nd essay, power and wisdom: politics as destiny. Kritika and Kontext, 3–4, 106–118

Derrida, J. 1982. Margins of philosophy. The University of Chicago Press, Chicago, IL, USA.

Deutsch, K.W. 1957. Political community and the North Atlantic area: international organization in the light of historical experience. Princeton University Press, Princeton, NJ, USA.

———— 1966. Nationalism and social communication: an inquiry into the foundations of nationality (2nd ed.). MIT Press, Cambridge, MA, USA.

———— 1988. The analysis of international relations (3rd ed.). Prentice-Hall, Englewood Cliffs, NJ, USA.

Docherty, T., ed. 1993. Postmodernism: a reader. Columbia University Press, New York, NY, USA.

Drucker, P.F. 1986. The changed world economy. Foreign Affairs, 64(4), 768–791.

Duverger, M. 1966. The idea of politics: the uses of power in society. Methuen, London, UK.

Easton, D. 1953. The political system: an inquiry into the state of political science. Alfred A. Knopf, New York, NY, USA.

Ellul, J. 1964. The technological society. Vintage, New York, NY, USA.

Elshtain, J.B. 1995. Democracy on trial. Basic Books, New York, NY, USA.

Esposito, J.L. 1992 The Islamic threat: myth or reality? Oxford University Press, Oxford, UK.

Fasching, D. 1981. The thought of Jacques Ellul: a systematic exposition. Edwin Mellen Press, New York, NY, USA.

Featherstone, M. 1990. Global culture, an introduction. Theory, Culture and Society, 7, 1–14.

Fisk, R. 1997. Threat, lies and videotape: reporting the Middle East. A public lecture, 18 Apr 1997, Carleton University, Ottawa, ON, Canada.

Foucault, M. 1965. Madness and civilization: a history of insanity in the Age of Reason. Pantheon, New York, NY, USA.

———— 1972. The archaeology of knowledge. Tavistock Publications, London, UK.

———— 1973. Birth of the clinic: an archaeology of medical perception. Pantheon Books, New York, NY, USA.

———— 1977. Discipline and punish. Pantheon, New York, NY, USA.

Fromm, E. 1968. The revolution of hope: toward a humanized technology. Harper and Row Publishers, New York, NY, USA.

Fukuyama, F. 1989. The end of history. The National Interest, 16 (Summer), 3–35.

——— 1992. The end of history and the last man. Free Press, New York, NY, USA.

——— 1999. The great disruption: human nature and the reconstitution of social order. The Atlantic Monthly, 283(5), 55–86.

Gaddis, J.L. 1999. Living in Candlestick Park. The Atlantic Monthly, 283(4), 65–74.

Gairdner, W.D., ed. 1998. After liberalism: essays in search of freedom, virtue, and order. Stoddart, Toronto, ON, Canada.

Garnett, J. 1984. Commonsense and the theory of international politics. State University of New York Press, Albany, NY, USA.

Gasset, J.O.Y. 1960. The revolt of the masses. Norton, New York, NY, USA.

GCON (Global Challenges and Opportunities Network). 1998. Policy Research Conference, 1–2 Oct, Ottawa, Canada. Policy Research Initiative, Government of Canada, Ottawa, ON, Canada. Internet: policyresearch.schoolnet.ca/networks/global/global-e.htm

Geertz, C. 1973. The interpretation of cultures. Basic, New York, NY, USA.

Gellner, E. 1983. Nations and nationalism. Cornell University Press, Ithaca, New York, NY, USA.

——— 1993. Postmodernism, reason and religion. Routledge, Chapman and Hall, Inc., New York, NY, USA.

Ghazali, M. 1978. Imam Ghazali's Ihya 'Ulum-id-din. 4 vols. Book Lovers Bureau, Lahore, Pakistan.

Gill, S. 1995. The global Panoptivon? The neoliberal state, economic life, and democratic surveillance. Alternatives, 2, 1–49.

Godelier, M. 1978. The concept of the "Asian mode of production" and Marxist models of social evolution. *In* Seddon, D., ed., Relations of production: Marxist approaches to economic anthropology. Cass, London, UK. pp. 209–257.

Gordon, A.; Ali, N.K.M. 1998. They shall not pass. Islamic Review (Jul–Aug). Internet: www.abim.com/majala/ireview

Gramsci, A. 1985. Selections from cultural writings. Lawrence and Wishart, London, UK.

Gress, D.R. 1997 The drama of modern Western identity. Orbis, 41(4), 525–544.

Grossberg, L.; Nelson, C.; Treichler, P., ed. 1992. Cultural studies. Routledge, Chapman and Hall, Inc., New York, NY, USA.

GSS (Group of Seven Summit). 1994. Summit communiqué, Jul 9. University of Toronto, Toronto, ON, Canada. Internet: www.library.utoronto.ca/g7/summit/1994naples/communique/index.html

Habermas, J. 1987. The philosophical discourse of modernity: twelve lectures. MIT Press, Cambridge, MA, USA.

——— 1992. The structure of the public sphere: an inquiry into a category of bourgeois society. MIT Press, Cambridge, MA, USA.

——— 1996. Further reflections on the public sphere. *In* Calhoun, C., ed., Habermas and the public sphere. MIT Press, Cambridge, MA, USA. pp. 421–461.

Halliday, F. 1979. Iran: dictatorship and development. Penguin Books, Harmondsworth, UK.

———— 1996. Islam and the myth of confrontation: religion and politics in the Middle East. I.B. Tauris, London, UK.

Hassan, I. 1985. The culture of postmodernism. Theory, Culture and Society, 2, 123–124.

Hegel, G. 1942. Hegel's *Philosophy of Right* (translated by T.M. Knox). Clarendon Press, Oxford, UK.

———— 1967. The phenomenology of mind (translated by J.B. Ballie). Harper and Row Publishers, New York, NY, USA.

Held, D. 1996. Models of democracy (2nd ed.). Stanford University Press, Stanford, CA, USA.

Helliwell, J. 1998. How much do national borders matter? The Brookings Institution, Washington, DC, USA.

Hobbes, T. [1651] 1968. Leviathan (edited with introduction by C.B. Macpherson). Penguin Books, New York, NY, USA.

Hobsbawm, E. 1990. Nations and nationalism since 1780. Cambridge University Press, Cambridge, UK.

———— 1996. The future of the state. *In* Hewitt de Alcantara, C., ed., Social futures, global visions. Blackwell, New York, NY, USA. pp. 55–66.

Hodgson, M.G.S. 1974. The venture of Islam: conscience and history in a world civilization. 3 vols. The University of Chicago Press, Chicago, IL, USA.

Hourani, A.H. 1991. A history of the Arab peoples. Faber and Faber, London, UK.

Hughes, G., ed. 1999. The politics of the soul: Eric Voegelin on religious experience. Rowman & Littlefield Publishers, Inc., Lanham, MD, USA.

Hunter, O.J. 1992. Technological literacy. Educational Technology, 32(3), 25–31.

Huntington, S. 1993. The clash of civilizations. Foreign Affairs, 73(3), 22–49.

———— 1996. The clash of civilizations and the remaking of world order. Simon & Schuster, New York, NY, USA.

———— 1997a. The clash of civilizations — a response. Millennium, 26(1), 141–142.

———— 1997b. The erosion of American national interest. Foreign Affairs, 76(5), 28–49.

Ibn Khaldun. 1958. The Muqaddimah: an introduction to history (translated by F. Rosenthal). 3 vols. Pantheon, New York, NY, USA.

Ibn Taymiyyah. 1966. Ibn Taimiyya on public and private law in Islam: or public policy in Islamic jurisprudence (translated by Omar A. Farrukh). Khayyats, Beirut, Lebanon.

Innis, H.A. 1951. The bias of communication. The University of Toronto Press, Toronto, ON, Canada.

Iqbal, S.M. 1951. The reconstruction of religious thought in Islam. Muhammad Ashraf Co., Lahore, Pakistan.

Jalal ad-Din Rumi. 1977. Mathnawi of Jalalu'ddin Rumi (translation and commentary by R.A. Nicholson). 3 vols. E.J.W. Gibb Memorial, London, UK.

Jaspers, K. 1957. Philosophical autobiography. In Schilpp, P.A., ed., The philosophy of Karl Jaspers. Tudor, New York, NY, USA. pp. 5–94.

Johnson, B.D. 1999. The second coming: as the newest Star Wars film illustrates, pop culture has become a new religion. Maclean's, 24 May, pp. 14–18.

Kaplan, A. 1964. The conduct of inquiry. Chandler, San Francisco, CA, USA.

Kaplan, R.D. 1994. The coming of anarchy. The Atlantic Monthly, 273(2), 44–76.

Kasra'i, S. 1999. Az khun-e Siyavash. Sokhan Publishing House, Tehran, Iran. [In Persian]

Kennan, G. (Mr X). 1947. The sources of Soviet conduct. Foreign Affairs, 25(4), 566–582.

Kepel, G. 1985. The prophet and pharaoh: Muslim extremism in Egypt. Al Saqi Books, London, UK.

Kung, H. 1990. Towards a world ethic of world religions, fundamental questions of present-day ethics in a global context. In Kung, H.; Moltmann, J., ed., The ethics of world religions and human rights. Concilium, New York, NY, USA. pp. 102–119.

————— 1992. Global responsibility: in search of a new world ethic. Continuum, New York, NY, USA.

————— 1994. Infallible? An unresolved inquiry. Continuum, New York, NY, USA.

————— 1996. Yes to a global ethic. Continuum, New York, NY, USA.

Landes, J.B., ed. 1998. Feminism, the public and the private. Oxford University Press, Oxford, UK.

Lawrence, B.B. 1989. Defenders of God: the fundamentalist revolt against the modern age. Harper and Row Publishers, San Francisco, CA, USA.

Linklater, A. 1998. The transformation of political community: ethical foundations of the post-Westphalian era. Polity Press, Oxford, UK.

Lippmann, W. 1956. The public philosophy. Mentor Books, New York, NY, USA.

Lisensky, R.P.; Pfnister, A.; Sweet, S.D. 1985. The new liberal learning: technology and the liberal arts. Council of Independent Colleges, Washington, DC, USA.

Lyotard, J.F. 1964. The postmodern condition: a report on knowledge (translated by G. Bennington and B. Massumi). University of Minneapolis Press, Minneapolis, MN, USA.

Mahdi, M. 1957. Ibn Khaldun's philosophy of history: a study in the philosophic foundation of the science of culture. Allen Books, London, UK.

Makdisi, G. 1990. The rise of humanism in classical Islam and the Christian West, with special reference to scholasticism. Edinburgh University Press, Edinburgh, UK.

Marcuse, H. 1964. One-dimensional man: studies in the ideology of advanced industrial society. Beacon Press, Boston, MA, USA.

Markoff, J. 1995. If medium is the message, the message is the Web. New York Times, 20 Nov, pp. A1 and D5.

Marx, K.; Engels, F. 1973. The communist manifesto (with an introduction by A.J.P. Taylor). Penguin Books, New York, NY, USA.

Maslow, A.H. 1970. Motivation and personality (2nd ed.). Harper and Row Publishers, New York, NY, USA.

Masuda, Y. 1990. Managing in the information society: releasing synergy Japanese style (2nd ed.). Blackwell, Oxford, UK.

McClelland, C.A. 1969. International relations: wisdom or science (rev. ed.). In Rosenau, J., ed., International politics and foreign policy: a reader in research and theory. Free Press, New York, NY, USA. pp. 3–5.

McLuhan, M. 1989. The global village: transformations in world life and media in the 21st century. Oxford University Press, New York, NY, USA.

McNeill, W.H. 1963. The rise of the West: a history of the human community. The University of Chicago Press, Chicago, IL, USA.

———— 1997. What we mean by the West. Orbis, 41(4), 513–524.

MCP (Members of the Clever Project). 1999. Hypersearching the web. Scientific American, 280(6), 54–60.

Meadows, D.H. 1972. The limits to growth: a report for the Club of Rome's project on the Predicament of Mankind. Universe, New York, NY, USA.

Meineche, F. 1957. Machiavellism: the doctrine of raison d'État and its place in modern history. Routledge, Chapman and Hall, Inc., London, UK.

Mill, J.S. 1949. Utilitarianism. Liberal Arts, New York, NY, USA.

Morgenthau, H. 1946. Scientific man vs. power politics. The University of Chicago Press, Chicago, IL, USA.

———— 1985. Politics among nations: struggle for power and peace (5th ed., rev.). Alfred A. Knopf, New York, NY, USA.

Moussalli, A. 1992. Radical Islamic fundamentalism: the ideological and political discourse of Sayyid Qutb. American University of Beirut, Beirut, Lebanon.

Mozaffari, M. 1998a. Can a declined civilization be re-constructed? Paper presented at the 3rd Pan-European International Relations Conference and Joint Meeting with the International Studies Association, 16–19 Sep, Vienna, Austria. International Studies Association, University of Arizona, Tucson, AZ, USA.

———— 1998b. Fatwa: violence and discourtesy. Aarhus University Press, Aarhus, Denmark.

Nasr, S.H. 1981. Knowledge and the sacred. Edinburgh University Press, Edinburgh, UK.

Neufeld, M. 1995. The restructuring of international relations theory. Cambridge University Press, Cambridge, UK.

Niebuhr, R. 1932. Moral man and immoral society: a study in ethics and politics. Charles Scribner's Sons, New York, NY, USA.

Oakeshott, M. 1989. The voice of liberal learning. Yale University Press, New Haven, CT, USA.

O'Brien, R. 1992. Global financial integration: the end of geography. Royal Institute of International Affairs, London, UK.

Orwell, G. 1949. Nineteen eighty-four, a novel. Secker & Warburg, London, UK.

Piscatori, J.A. 1986. Islam in a world of nation-states. Cambridge University Press, Cambridge, UK.
——— 1991. Islamic fundamentalisms and the Gulf crisis. Fundamentalism Project; American Academy of Arts and Sciences, Chicago, IL, USA.
Plato. 1948. The Republic of Plato [translated by Alan Bloom]. Basic Books, New York, NY, USA.
Polanyi, K. 1944. The great transformation. Beacon Press, Boston, MA, USA.
Postman, N. 1992. Technopoly: the surrender of culture to technology. Alfred A. Knopf, New York, NY, USA.

RAC (Race and Class). 1998–99. The threat of globalism (special issue). Race and Class, a Journal for Black and Third World Liberation, 40(2–3).
Rajaee, F. 1993. Tahavol Andisheye Siyassi dar Sharqe Bastan [The development of political ideas in the ancient East]. Qumes, Tehran, Iran.
——— 1994. Intellectuals and culture: guardians of traditions or vanguards of development. In Soemardjan, S.; Thompson, K.W., ed., Culture, development, and democracy, the role of the intellectuals. United Nations University Press, New York, NY, USA. pp. 39–52.
——— 1997. Ma'rekeye Jahanbiniha: dar Kheradvarziye Siyassi va Hoviyate Ma Iranian [The battle of world views: on political rationalism and our Iranian identity] (2nd ed.). Ehya Ketab, Tehran, Iran.
——— 1998. On liberty: Isaiah Berlin and his legacy. Political and Economic Ettela'at, 11(125–126), 20–23.
——— 1999. A Thermidor of Islamic yuppies? Conflict and compromise in Iran's politics. Middle East Journal, 53(2), 217–231.
Rauscher, M. 1989. OPEC and the price of petroleum: theoritical considerations and empirical evidence. Springer-Verlag, Berlin, Germany.
Rawls, J. 1971. A theory of justice. Harvard University Press, Cambridge, MA, USA.
——— 1993. The law of peoples. Critical Inquiry, 20(I), 36–68.
Riggs, F.W. 1964. Administration in developing countries: the theory of prismatic society. Mifflin, Boston, MA, USA.
——— 1973. Prismatic society revisited. General Learning Press, Morristown, NJ, USA.
Robertson, R. 1992. Globalization: social theory and global culture. Sage, London, UK.
Rosenau, J. 1998. Global affairs in an epochal transformation. In Rayan, H.; Peartree, E., ed., The information revolution and international security. Center for Strategic and International Studies Press, Washington, DC, USA. pp. 31–57.
Ryan, S.J.W.S. 1995. Culture, spirituality, and economic development: opening a dialogue. International Development Research Centre, Ottawa, ON, Canada.

Sa'di, M. 1979. The rose-garden of Sheikh Muslihu'd-din Sadi of Shiraz (translated by E.B. Eastwick). Octagon, London, UK.
Said, E.W. 1978. Orientalism. Vintage Books, New York, NY, USA.

———— 1993. Culture and imperialism. Alfred A. Knopf, New York, NY, USA.

———— 1998. Bridge across the abyss. Al Ahram Weekly, 394, Cairo, 10–16 Sep, pp. 4ff.

Samuelson, R. 1998. Asian boom + Asian crisis = total mystery. International Herald Tribune, 20 Mar, p. 12.

Sayer, D. 1991. Capitalism and modernity: an excursus on Marx and Weber. Routledge, Chapman and Hall, Inc., London, UK.

Scarre, G. 1996. Utilitarianism. Routlege, Chapman and Hall, Inc., London, UK.

Shariati, A. [1362] 1982. Majmueye Asar, Bazgasht [The conception of return]. Vol. 4 of collection. Nashr Asar, Terhran, Iran.

Shaw, M. 1997. The state and globalization: towards a theory of state transformation. Review of International Political Economy, 4(3), 497–513.

Shiva, V. 1993. Monocultures of the mind: perspectives on biodiversity and biotechnology. Zed Books, London, UK.

SIPRI (Stockholm International Peace Research Institute). 1996. 1996 yearbook, armaments, disarmament and international security. Oxford University Press, Oxford, UK.

Sivananda, A. 1998–99. Globalism and the left. Race and Class, a Journal for Black and Third World Liberation, 40(2–3), 5–19.

Snow, C.P. 1959. Two cultures and the scientific revolution. Cambridge University Press, Cambridge, UK.

Spragens, T., Jr. 1976. Understanding political theories. St Martin's Press, New York, NY, USA.

Statistics Canada. 1997. Canada year book 1997. Industry Canada, Ottawa, ON, Canada.

Stone, L. 1979. The family, sex and marriage in England (abridged ed.). Harper and Row, New York, NY, USA.

Strauss, L. 1958. Thoughts on Machiavelli. The University of Chicago Press, Chicago, IL, USA.

———— 1959. What is political philosophy? and other essays. The Free Press, Glencoe, IL, USA.

Tagliabue, J. 1998. In Europe, steps toward a common language. New York Times, 19 Jul, pp. 1 and 4.

Taqizadeh, S.H. 1920. Tajjadod [Modernity]. Kaveh, 1, Berlin, 22 Jan, pp. 1ff.

Taylor, F.W. 1947. Scientific management: comprising shop management, the principle of scientific management and testimony before the Special House Committee. Harper and Row Publishers, New York, NY, USA.

Tonnies, F. 1955. Community and association. Routledge and Kegan Paul, London, UK.

Toynbee, A. 1934. A study of history. 10 vols. Oxford University Press, London, UK.

Toynbee, A.J.; Caplan, J. 1972. A study of history: a new edition revised and abridged. Oxford University Press, London, UK.

UNESCO (United Nations Educational, Scientific and Cultural Organization). 1995. Our creative diversity: report of the World Commission on Culture and Development. UNESCO Publishing, Paris, France.

Voegelin, E. 1952. The new science of politics: an introduction. The University of Chicago Press, Chicago, IL, USA.
———— 1956. Order and history. Vol. 2: The world of the polis. Louisiana State University Press, Baton Rouge, LA, USA.

Walker, R.B.J. 1988. One world, many worlds: struggles for a just world peace. Lynne Rienner Publishers, Boulder, CO, USA.
———— 1993. Inside/outside: international relations as political theory. Cambridge University Press, Cambridge, UK.
Weber, M. 1958a. Politics as a vocation. In C.W. Mills, ed., From Max Weber: essays in sociology. Oxford University Press, New York, NY, USA. pp. 77–128.
———— 1958b. The Protestant ethic and the spirit of capitalism. Scribner and Sons, New York, NY, USA.
Weidenbaum, M. 1994–95. The business response to the global marketplace. In Annual edition: world politics. Dushkin Publishing Group, Inc., Guiford, CT, USA. pp. 186–192.
Weizenbaum, J. 1976. Computer power and human reason: from judgment to calculation. W.H. Freeman and Company, San Francisco, CA, USA.
Wilkinson, J. 1964. Jacques Ellul as the philosopher of the technological society. In Ellul, J., ed., The technological society. Vintage Books, New York, NY, USA. pp. ix–xx.
Wilson, E.O. 1998. Consilience. the unity of knowledge. Alfred A. Knopf, New York, NY, USA.
Wriston, W.B. 1992. The twilight of sovereignty: how the information revolution is transforming our world. Charles Scribner's & Son, New York, NY, USA.

Zakaria, F. 1997. The rise of illiberal democracy. Foreign Affairs, 76(6), 22–43.

OTHER READING

Amin, S. 1989. Eurocentrism. Monthly Review, New York, NY, USA.
Ansell-Pearson, K. 1994. An introduction to Nietzsche as political thinker. Cambridge University Press, Cambridge, UK.

Berlin, I. 1969. Four essays on liberty. Oxford University Press, London, UK.
Berman, M. 1988. All that is solid melts into air: the experience of modernity. Penguin Books, New York, NY, USA.
Bernal, M. 1987. Black Athena: the Afroasiatic roots of classical civilization. Free Association Books, London, UK.
Berry, B.; Lobley, J.; Conkling, E.C.; Ray, D.M. 1997. The global economy in transition (rev. ed.). Prentice-Hall, Upper Saddle River, NJ, USA.

Buck, S.J. 1998. The global commons: an introduction. Island Press, Washington, DC, USA.

Castells, M. 1994. Technopoles of the world: the making of twenty-first-century industrial complexes. Routledge, Chapman and Hall, Inc., London, UK.
———— 1998. End of millennium. Blackwell, Malden, MA, USA.
Cornford, F.M. 1957. From religion to philosophy. Harper and Row Publishers, New York, NY, USA.
Council of Europe. 1998. Virtual new world?: debates. Council of Europe Press, Strasbourg, France.

Dahrendorf, R. 1997. After 1989: morals, revolution and civil society. St Martin's Press, New York, NY, USA.
Drucker, P.F. 1950. The new society: the anatomy of the industrial order. Harper and Row Publishers, New York, NY, USA.
———— 1992. Managing the future: the 1990s and beyond. Dutton, New York, NY, USA.
———— 1993. Post-capitalist society. HarperBusiness, New York, NY, USA.

Elias, N. 1994. The civilizing process: the history of manners and state formation and civilization. Blackwell, Oxford, UK.
Ellul, J. 1980. The technological system. Continuum, New York, NY, USA.

Falk, R. 1993. The making of global citizenship. In Brecher, J.; Childs, J.B.; Cutler, J., ed., Global visions: beyond the new world order. South End Press, Boston, MA, USA.
Franklin, U.M. 1992. The real world of technology. House of Anansi Press, Concord, ON, Canada.

Grant, G. 1969. Technology and empire: reflections on North America. House of Anansi, Toronto, ON, Canada.

Held, D. 1995. Democracy and global order: from modern state to cosmopolitan governance. Polity Press, Cambridge, UK.

Innis, H.A. 1986. Empire and communications. P. Porcepic, Victoria, BC, Canada.

Leebaert, D. 1991. Technology 2001: the future of computing and communications. MIT Press, Cambridge, MA, USA.
Lefkowitz, M.R.; Rogers, G.M. 1996. Black Athena revisited. University of North Carolina Press, Chapel Hill, NC, USA.

Masuda, Y. 1980. The information society. Institute for the Information Society, Tokyo, Japan.
Mitcham, C. 1994. Thinking through technology: the path between engineering and philosophy. The University of Chicago Press, Chicago, IL, USA.

143

Mittelman, J.H., ed. 1996. Globalization: critical reflections. Lynne Rienner Publishers, Boulder, CO, USA.

Nasr, S.H. 1996. Religion and the order of nature. Oxford University Press, New York, NY, USA.
Nietzsche, F. 1990. Beyond good and evil. Penguin Books, New York, NY, USA.

Reich, R. 1992. The work of nations: preparing ourselves for the 21st century (new ed.). Vintage Press, New York, NY, USA.
Robertson, R. 1992. Globalization: social theory and global culture. Sage, London, UK.

Sen, A.K. 1992. Inequality reexamined. Russell Sage Foundation, New York, NY, USA.
Snarr, M.T.; Snarr, D.N., ed. 1999. Introducing global issues. Lynne Rienner Publishers, Boulder, CO, USA.
Splichal, S.; Calabrese, A.; Sparks, C., ed. 1994. Information society and civil society: contemporary perspectives on the changing world order. Purdue University Press, West Lafayette, IN, USA.

Tehranian, M. 1999. Global communication and world politics: domination, development, and discourse. Lynne Rienner Publishers, Boulder, CO, USA.

Index

n indicates footnote; t indicates table

147

ABOUT THE AUTHOR

Professor Farhang Rajaee is a Visiting Associate Professor in the College of the Humanities at Carleton University, Ottawa, Canada. Professor Rajaee received his PhD in foreign affairs in 1983 from the University of Virginia, where he worked with Kenneth W. Thompson and Inis Claude, Jr. In 1984, he served on the Iranian United Nations delegation and, from 1985 to 1996, taught at the University of Tehran, the Iranian Academy of Philosophy, and Beheshti (National) University. In 1990 and 1991, Professor Rajaee was a Fellow of Oxford University and a Research Fellow in 1996 at the Zentrum Moderner Orient in Berlin. He is the author of many articles and books, including *The Development of Political Thought in the Ancient East* (Tehran 1993) and *The Battle of Worldviews* (Tehran, 1995 and 1997).